Extravagant Love:
The Call And Response To
God's Grace

I0149844

Cycle B Sermons For Lent And Easter
Based On The Second Readings

Karna Moskalik

CSS Publishing Company, Inc.
Lima, Ohio

EXTRAVAGANT LOVE: THE CALL AND RESPONSE TO GOD'S GRACE

FIRST EDITION
Copyright © 2023
by CSS Publishing Co., Inc.

Library of Congress Cataloging-in-Publication Data:

Names: Moskalik, Karna, author.
Title: Extravagant love: the call and response to God's grace : cycle B
   sermons for Lent and Easter based on the second readings / Karna
   Moskalik.
Description: First edition. | Lima, Ohio : CSS Publishing Company, Inc.,
   [2023]
Identifiers: LCCN 2023004918 (print) | LCCN 2023004919 (ebook) | ISBN
   9780788030840 | ISBN 9780788030857 (ebook)
Subjects: LCSH: Love--Biblical teaching. | God--Love--Biblical teaching. |
   God--Worship and love--Biblical teaching. | Bible. New
   Testament--Criticism, interpretation, etc.
Classification: LCC BS680.L64 M68 2023 (print) | LCC BS680.L64 (ebook) |
   DDC 252/.62--dc23/eng/20230701
LC record available at https://lccn.loc.gov/2023004918
LC ebook record available at https://lccn.loc.gov/2023004919

For more information about CSS Publishing Company resources, visit our website at www.csspub.com, email us at csr@csspub.com, or call (800) 241-4056.

e-book:
ISBN-13: 978-0-7880-3085-7
ISBN-10: 0-7880-3085-X

ISBN-13: 978-0-7880-3084-0
ISBN-10: 0-7880-3084-1   PRINTED IN USA

Contents

Foreword 5

Acknowledgments 6

Ash Wednesday: 2 Corinthians 5:20b--6:10
A Love That Heals Deep Wounds 9

First Sunday in Lent: 1 Peter 3:18-22
A Love That Forgives And Frees 14

Second Sunday in Lent: Romans 4:13-25
A Love That Never Fails 18

Third Sunday in Lent: 1 Corinthians 1:18-25
A Love That Heals Divisions 23

Fourth Sunday in Lent: Ephesians 2:1-10
An Unconditional Love 28

Fifth Sunday in Lent: Hebrews 5:5-10
A Love Becoming 32

Liturgy of the Passion: Philippians 2:5-11
The Journey Of Love 35

Maundy Thursday: 1 Corinthians 11:23-26
A Love That Calls You By Name 38

Good Friday: Hebrews 10:16-25
A Love Amidst Life's Questions 41

Resurrection of the Lord: Acts 10:34-43
An Extravagant Love For The World 44

Second Sunday of Easter: 1 John 1:1-2:2
A Love That Shines 48

Third Sunday of Easter: 1 John 3:1-7
A Love That Claims And Names Us 52

Fourth Sunday of Easter: 1 John 3:16-24
Love Is A Verb 56

Fifth Sunday of Easter: 1 John 4:7-21
God Is Love 60

Sixth Sunday of Easter: 1 John 5:1-6
Love One Another 64

Seventh Sunday of Easter: 1 John 5:9-13
A Life Of Love 68

Day of Pentecost: Acts 2:1-20
Share The Love 72

About The Author 77

Foreword

"All You Need is Love," a popular song from the Beatles, sings a great truth: All of humanity longs to be truly known and loved unconditionally. We are a walking wounded in search of healing and wholeness. Where do we find an extravagant love that embraces fully?

In our divided society, loving one's neighbor is a rare feature article. Instead, the headline news creates further anxiety as we encounter stories of war, disease and polarizing politics. It is in the midst of this broken and fractured world that Jesus would show us a more excellent way: *love*. The authors of the New Testament letters were transformed by this divine love. Jesus came to heal our wounded souls, and empower us to abundantly share this grace with a hurting world.

God's love is eternal. From the beginning of creation, throughout the Old and New Testament and into today's world, God keeps the promise of pouring forth this extravagant love. The letters in the New Testament speak of a profound love of God that brings healing of deep wounds, and the empowerment to live out our calling to love the neighbor in need.

At a very young and impressionable age, I sensed God call me by name through the Christian community. Whenever the congregation recited the Nicene Creed on communion Sunday's, I was in awe at the phrase, "He became *incarnate* and was made man." In my innocence, I mistakenly heard, "He became '*in-Karna*.'" My impressionable young ears heard a mysterious call from a loving God.

The beloved disciple John reminds us that "we love because Christ first loved us" (1 John 4:19). May you trust in God's overflowing grace in your life and answer the call to be Jesus' loving presence in today's world. God's love for all of us is *extravagant*. May we all feel the embrace of God and share this Good News with a world so hungry for Christ's love.

Acknowledgments

God richly blessed me with a cloud of witnesses that nurtured my faith. My parents, Maury and Kathy, shared their love of Jesus with my two brothers Eric and Ethan and me. Many mentors, congregations, Bible camps, The Minnesota All-State Lutheran Choir, Youth Encounter, and campus ministry organizations inspired my walk with God. I offer a special thank you to the congregations I've served as youth minister, intern, and as pastor. I am especially grateful for my call to Our Savior's Lutheran in Stillwater. This congregation defines itself as a "caring community," in our mission statement. Our Savior's generously lives out our calling to demonstrate God's love to all.

Most of all, thank you to my husband Brian for his deep love and joyful personality. The extravagant love of Jesus is so apparent through the many people that I've met along life's journey. Thanks be to God.

This book is dedicated to my loving husband Brian Moskalik. Your love is extravagant. God answered my prayers when you came into my life. Thank you for showing me a life of joy and abundance. I am forever grateful for your support and encouragement.

A Love That Heals Deep Wounds

So we are ambassadors for Christ, since God is making his appeal through us; we entreat you on behalf of Christ, be reconciled to God. For our sake he made him to be sin who knew no sin, so that in him we might become the righteousness of God. As we work together with him, we urge you also not to accept the grace of God in vain. For he says, 'At an acceptable time I have listened to you, and on a day of salvation I have helped you.' See, now is the acceptable time; see, now is the day of salvation! We are putting no obstacle in anyone's way, so that no fault may be found with our ministry, but as servants of God we have commended ourselves in every way: through great endurance, in afflictions, hardships, calamities, beatings, imprison-ments, riots, labors, sleepless nights, hunger; by purity, knowledge, patience, kindness, holiness of spirit, genuine love, truthful speech, and the power of God; with the weapons of righteousness for the right hand and for the left; in honor and dishonor, in ill repute and good repute. We are treated as impostors, and yet are true; as un-known, and yet are well known; as dying, and see — we are alive; as punished, and yet not killed; as sorrowful, yet always rejoicing; as poor, yet making many rich; as having nothing, and yet possessing everything.

It was February of 2019. One of my dearest friends was so full of anticipation. She had been dating her boyfriend for a few years, and she was convinced that a Valentine's Day marriage proposal would happen. My friend had gone through severe heartbreak earlier in her life. She felt confident about this relationship. In mid-February, my friend called me to share her devastation. The proposal did not come. She shared her new motto: "No one can love you harder than your-self." As she said these words, a strange peace came over her. She con-tinued to express, "Well, I can't have expectations of others. I am just going to love myself."

Doesn't this seem to be the way of human nature? It's easy to look out for number one and be suspicious of others. This is especially true in the United States. Our nephew André noticed this right away. He grew up in Mexico. As a dual citizen, André was fascinated to learn more about the history of the United States. During a government class, he learned a new English word. One day he asked me: "What does the word 'faction mean?" I began to describe how a "faction" means separation. He had read an essay by Thomas Paine that explained the potential for political divide in the development of the United States. Understanding the definition of "faction," André was able to comprehend the entire essay. We do live in a world of factions. We have witnessed this in the news media.

When we hear the word, "reconciled," often we may think of the very opposite reality. The phrase, "irreconcilable differences," crop up in marriages, politics and even churches. A separation and brokenness seems commonplace in our fractured world. Reconciliation is the opposite. Reconciliation brings two parties together. There is a restoring of a relationship that already exists. This is such a word of hope for our world today. Yet, how do we experience this reconnection? How can there be deep healing of wounds? It is too easy to continue severing. The easiest response is just to look out for number one. Perhaps adopting the motto, "No one can love you harder than yourself," is a big temptation.

This is why Paul wrote to the community of Corinth. He was hopeful that through the power of God's forgiveness, a broken church could find deep healing. Paul established the church in Corinth in about eighteen months. Just *four* months after his departure he discovered there were factions. There were divisions in the body of Christ. This prompted him to write First Corinthians. In this letter, he speaks in depth about what it means to be a healthy and whole body of Christ. First Corinthians 12 reminds us that the entire body: hands, feet, ears, and eyes, are all crucial members. No part is superior to another. All are essential. Then he continues to address in the next chapter of a more excellent way: *love.* First Corinthians was well-received by some, but not by others. There were still divisions. Paul makes reference to a, "letter of tears." Some scholars wonder if the tearful letter is the last few chapters of Second Corinthians, or if it was a lost letter all together. The community of Corinth not only had divisions, they also began to question Paul and his leadership. Who was he to intervene? By what authority did he speak that they should forgive and heal?

As the wealthy treated the poor with disdain and disrespect, there was even holy commotion when it came time for receiving the body and blood of Christ. The working class couldn't get to worship on time and often missed out on the sacrament. Debates also existed on eating food sacrificed to idols. The church was truly divided. They had forgotten what it meant to serve one another and show honor.

When you look at our larger world, or perhaps in your own personal relationships, irreconcilable differences may create feelings of hopelessness. This may also result in a lack of vision for the future. How can there be healing and a coming together? Paul offers a hopeful word about restoring relationships. He had total confidence that God can truly mend deep wounds. There is always hope. Paul knew this firsthand. He had experienced the ultimate reconciliation, and healing of deep wounds. His conversion story offers hope.

On the road to Damascus, Paul's life drastically changed. Upon meeting the risen Jesus, Paul transformed from the biggest *adversary* of Christianity to the biggest *advocate* of Christ's love. From murderer of believers, to risking the rest of his life to proclaim the good news everywhere, Paul knew that transformation was completely possible. Blinded for three days, he fasted. He prayed deeply and reflected on his life. While he prayed, Ananias, a follower of Jesus, was commissioned to lay healing hands on Saul. After some resistance, a true miracle happened. Ananias referred to Saul as, "brother," in the healing process. This healing moment transformed both of their lives. Saul would indeed become Paul — God's chosen instrument to lay the groundwork of planting churches and write inspiring letters of encouragement. Ananias could have ignored the Holy Spirit's nudge to bless Saul. Instead, Ananias follows through with blessing Paul and naming him as his "brother." He recognized the reality that we are all created in the image of God. They both recognized one another's humanity.

As Paul wrote in Second Corinthians, "be reconciled," this refers to more than church politics. He states, "Be reconciled — *to God*" (2 Corinthians 5:20b). How could they do that? How could they possibly be reconciled to God in the midst of their sin and turmoil and struggle? Paul continues to tell us how this is possible. Reconciliation is not based on their own works or merits, but based on the pure lavish love and grace of God.

Paul continues and says, "God made him who had no sin to be sin for us so that in him we might become the righteousness of God through the power of the Holy Spirit" (2 Corinthians 5:21). *God* brings reconciliation and repairing. The holy and the human would re-connect and be restored into a right relationship. This restoration heals and transforms us. This relationship mends even the most hopeless situations. Wounds that are impossible to heal are mended by Jesus, the Great Physician. This reconciliation is based on Christ's power and the transformative love of God. The verses before and after this reading provide a deepened context. In Second Corinthians 5:17, Paul offers encouragement: "For if anyone is in Christ they are a new creation. The old has passed. The new has come." Also the following verses in Second Corinthians 6:10 express a longing for an opened heart. Paul urges that a mutuality of open hearts be extended to each other in the congregation as well as to Paul.

Reconciliation is made possible through God's healing power and initiative. The happy exchange is a theological concept in which God takes on our sin and brokenness. Christ takes our wounds and makes us whole. This gives us God's righteousness and love. This is a happy exchange for *us*. Because of this transformation, Paul is now saying that we can be ambassadors. We are entrusted to reflect God's love in the world as servants. We are not to let this ministry be discounted or questioned. Perseverance through hardships may reveal God's love to a divided world. We begin to reflect this forgiving, renewing love of Jesus to those who feel scorned and separated from community.

The motto, "no one can love you harder than yourself," I would have to disagree with this statement. While we as humans fail at perfecting love, I am reminded of a game my niece and I played when she was around four years old. This playful dialogue would make English teachers cringe. My niece would express, "I love you Auntie Karna." I would chime back, "I love you more." My niece would say, "I love you more-er!" Not to be outdone, I would create a sort of game out of this exchange and say, "I love you more-er-est!" We would then continue going back and forth adding "er" and "est" until we got lost. Finally, my little niece would say, "not possible!" While this is a cute conversation with a child, it reminds me of an important reality. When it comes to our relationship with God, *all* things are possible. Wounds can be made whole. Life can be full of hope and transformation.

I'm also happy to report that my dear friend who was so full of disappointment in February of 2019, received her proposal later that year in June. "No one can love you harder than yourself — " that might be true from a human standpoint. From a Godly standpoint there is one that can love you more fiercely and perfectly than anyone else. The love of Christ transforms us, makes us new, and sets us on the right path. As we are transformed by that love, we bear witness to it in the world in our daily lives. There is hope in your life. There's hope even for our country. There's hope for the world. Our hope comes from the love and grace of God. Amen.

A Love That Forgives And Frees

For Christ also suffered for sins once for all, the righteous for the unrighteous, in order to bring you to God. He was put to death in the flesh, but made alive in the spirit, in which also he went and made a proclamation to the spirits in prison, who in former times did not obey, when God waited patiently in the days of Noah, during the building of the ark, in which a few, that is, eight people, were saved through water. And baptism, which this prefigured, now saves you — not as a removal of dirt from the body, but as an appeal to God for a good conscience, through the resurrection of Jesus Christ, who has gone into heaven and is at the right hand of God, with angels, authorities, and powers made subject to him.

There is a national holiday that has been celebrated since the end of the Civil War: Juneteenth. This marks the end of slavery that was practiced in the United States when the last slaves in Texas discovered they were indeed free. God wants all of us to live in freedom. Yet we know that not all experience liberation. Systemic racism perpetuates a suppression of voices. The sin of racism holds us all captive. God desires that we reclaim the theological affirmation of the Imago Dei. That is, we are all created in the image of God.

Perhaps you were stunned when George Floyd died in 2020 when a police officer kneeled on his neck for multiple minutes. This event enraged people throughout the world. This tragic death happened just 25 miles away from our congregation, Our Savior's in Stillwater, Minnesota. When we fully know our own stories and the stories of others, this fills us with greater understanding and compassion. Since George Floyd's untimely death, I have read multiple books on understanding racism. As a congregation, we also spent the summer of 2020 reading together the book, *Waking Up White*, by Debby Irving. We also put our faith into action and offered relief supplies of food and water after riots enflamed the Twin Cities neighborhoods.

As we continue to reflect on our history as a nation, and how to work toward racial justice, my book club read a novel that I highly recommend called *Home Going*, by Yaa Gyasi. This novel depicts a storyline of two half-sisters from Ghana. The story chronicles how one was sold into slavery, while the other stayed in Ghana. The sisters didn't even know the other one existed. As the novel progresses, seven future generations, relatives of the sisters, all shed light on the sin of racism and the societal challenges of each passing decade. It was a painful book to read, but it really was eye-opening for me to see what people have experienced in our own country and throughout the world. We live in a world that is broken. This violence may often overwhelm us too.

In this powerful passage from First Peter in the third chapter, the very first verse caught my attention: "For Christ suffered *once*" (1 Peter 3:18). This was the suffering on the cross. Christ who knew no sin would take on the sins and suffering and pain of the whole world. All that had happened before, present and future would be met on the cross. Jesus would do this out of his deep love for all people. Christ suffered once for all the sins of all time on the cross.

In reflection on racism — a sin passed on through generations — we recognize that we are in *bondage* to sin. We *need* Christ to set us free. We are caught in a generational web of systemic racism. Christ suffered once for all. Humanity continues to suffer.

This letter that Peter writes is quite compelling — because he was writing to a *suffering church*. The early believers were persecuted by the Emperor Nero. Peter was also writing to an entire region of believers, rather than a single congregation. The recipients of this letter included all of Asia Minor, such as, Cappadocia, Pontus, Galatia, and Bithynia. This is the region today of modern Turkey. When Second Peter was written, this was considered a farewell letter. Peter is offering encouragement in the midst of suffering and persecution.

We can be bound by the sins of others in persecution. Racism is one clear example of a societal sin. However, *some sins are **self-inflicted***. Sometimes we are caught in ***our own cycles*** that replay over and over again. Peter's personal story reveals that he was acquainted with ***personal*** and ***self-inflicted*** wounds. When Peter had denied friendship with Jesus, he felt such a weight on his conscience. He didn't even feel worthy to be considered a disciple. Jesus knew that Peter felt as if his sins were unforgivable. As Jesus rose from the grave he made sure that he told the women to go tell the disciples "and Peter," (Mark 16:7). He wanted to reassure Peter that he was *still* a disciple. Peter felt burdened by his own failings. Peter was afraid that this was a defining moment in his life. He didn't see much of a future past that moment. Yet, Jesus, out of his grace, compassion and love, takes Peter aside. Just as Peter denied Christ three times, Jesus welcomes him with arms of love and grace with a threefold ask: do you love me? In other words, Jesus was indicating that Peter would still be the rock upon which Jesus would build the church.

Peter was set free from the imprisonment of his mind. That freedom inspired him to proclaim grace to others. First Peter 3:19 states that Jesus suffered *once* for our sins on the cross, and then Christ "made proclamation to the *imprisoned spirits.*" Isn't that an interesting phrase? *Imprisoned spirits* paints this image of being bound up, and in need of emancipation. This freedom comes from Christ alone.

Jesus sets us free from imprisonment through God's grace on the cross. We are assured of God's gracious new life through the waters of our baptisms. First Peter 3 also reminds us of the power of the flood and Noah's story. Water may cleanse, destroy, and refresh. It is essential to sustaining life. As God wanted to write a new story with Noah, God writes a news story with Jesus. We are set free and forgiven because of what Christ has done. We are forgiven and cleansed in the waters of baptism. We know that we are children of God. Yet, we perpetually fall into sin. We are captive to sin and cannot free ourselves. The cross and the empty tomb proclaim the promise of everlasting life. Our baptismal waters restore us to new and abundant life in Christ. There is good news that we are beloved children of God, forgiven and freed in the waters of baptism.

Children seem to know this abundant freedom in Christ. I once led a milestone ministry devotion for seventeen three-year-olds. It was like herding cats to get them all in the same location. As we circled around the baptismal font, I asked the children: "Where have you seen this before?" One child genuinely responded, "This is a wishing well. I saw this at a mall!" Another youngster so innocently corrected him saying, "That's not a wishing well. That's a *bath*-tism!" Like water, the faith of children is so refreshing. The baptismal waters cleanse us, drown our old sinful self, and raise us to a new life of freedom. We are made clean in our *"bath-tism."*

What would our world look like if we took our baptismal claims seriously? As we are anchored in our identities as God's beloved children, the gracious flow of God's healing and living waters transforms the world. Martin Luther, the great reformer, reminds us of the *Freedom of a Christian*. Trusting in the promises of God that we are truly loved, forgiven and freed, this empowers us to abundantly proclaim freedom to *everyone*. We are commissioned to serve others joyfully. We are set free. We are called to share this liberating gospel to a world that often feels *imprisoned*. Rather than perpetuating endless cycles of persecution, we are held in the healing embrace of Jesus who suffered *once*. We are extravagantly loved and held in this holy embrace.

Peter was stuck in his own mind replaying events from his past. Peter needed to be reminded that he's forgiven and freed. We also know that *we* are forgiven and freed. As God writes a new story with Jesus, so God writes a new story with all of us today. We are Christians, *"little Christ's,"* proclaiming God's love in words and actions. We are *set free* to love our neighbors. As you experience God's grace first hand, let that love pour forth to bless others.

We might not be able to change history and generations of pain from systemic racism. However, we can write a new chapter. Our pathway forward can look differently. When we experience this freedom through Christ's victory on the cross, and the healing waters claiming us in our baptisms, this liberates us to love and serve our neighbors. May we continue to work toward social justice in all forms. May we learn and grow as a community, as a country and as a world. May we experience this transformational love of God that changes us and has the power to change everyone. We are forgiven. We are free. God bless, Amen.

A Love That Never Fails

For the promise that he would inherit the world did not come to Abraham or to his descendants through the law but through the righteousness of faith. If it is the adherents of the law who are to be the heirs, faith is null and the promise is void. For the law brings wrath; but where there is no law, neither is there violation. For this reason it depends on faith, in order that the promise may rest on grace and be guaranteed to all his descendants, not only to the adherents of the law but also to those who share the faith of Abraham (for he is the father of all of us, as it is written, 'I have made you the father of many nations') — in the presence of the God in whom he believed, who gives life to the dead and calls into existence the things that do not exist. Hoping against hope, he believed that he would become 'the father of many nations', according to what was said, 'So numerous shall your descendants be.' He did not weaken in faith when he considered his own body, which was already as good as dead (for he was about a hundred years old), or when he considered the barrenness of Sarah's womb. No distrust made him waver concerning the promise of God, but he grew strong in his faith as he gave glory to God, being fully convinced that God was able to do what he had promised. Therefore his faith 'was reckoned to him as righteousness.' Now the words, 'it was reckoned to him', were written not for his sake alone, but for ours also. It will be reckoned to us who believe in him who raised Jesus our Lord from the dead, who was handed over to death for our trespasses and was raised for our justification.

One of the amenities that I love about Stillwater is the bike trails. During the summertime, it is a joy to awaken early in the morning and ride the "bridge loop." This is a fourteen-mile round trip journey from my home. Entering into downtown Stillwater, across the St. Croix River, and into Wisconsin and back to Minnesota, is a great morning fitness routine. The steep hill climbs in the river valley provide gorgeous scenery. Often I think to myself when I bike in such a scenic surrounding, "there is so much joy in the journey."

Truthfully, there isn't always joy when it comes to the journey of life. There may be potholes, detours, and hill climbs that are too challenging. Sometimes in life's journey, we may have flat tires or we are simply out of gas to press forward. Last summer, while I was biking for a cycling event held in Stillwater, I had the most unusual experience. After over a decade of distance cycling, somehow I got stuck in a gear. In that moment, with my clipped in cycling shoes, I almost tipped over. I couldn't move forward. Instead, I was absolutely stuck. My pedals could not propel forward or backward. I was immobilized. Unfortunately, I also did not know what to do to solve the situation.

Sometimes, in our discipleship, we may also find moments in which we become stuck. A tragedy happens in the wider world or in our own lives that stirs doubt. We may not know what to do to make this world safe and just. Maybe you feel stuck right now as you hear news reports. School shootings of elementary aged children break our hearts. Recently, a 6.1 magnitude earthquake killed over 1,000 people in Afghanistan. There is also a continual fracturing in our political system requiring healing.

Perhaps what immobilizes you in your faith life is a personal struggle. Maybe you have been stuck for years — asking the bigger questions and wondering where God is in the midst of the journey. When this happens, there is a temptation to fall prey to something called, "reductionism." That is, we reduce God. We assume that God is too small and that nothing can alleviate the pain or allow life to make sense. When our world feels like it's collapsing on us we make God too small. When we find ourselves in this faith crisis, we may begin to question who God is, and even the character of God. Will God be faithful? Will God truly keep promises?

The book of Romans has a lot of hope to offer those that are experiencing a faith crisis. The scripture for today highlights Abraham and the complexities of his faith journey. While God is faithful and did keep promises for Abraham, it is also inspiring to know that many heavyweight theologians have read the book of Romans through the years and found it to be a strong foundation to re-construct their faith.

St. Augustine assumed that God's grace could not possibly cover the multitude of sins that he committed. One day, Augustine sensed God's presence urging him to, "take up and read," as he overheard children playing outside. On his countertop was the book of Romans.

As he began to dwell in the promises found in the scriptures, he realized that God is truly gracious. God's extravagant love became abundantly clear to Augustine.

In a similar fashion, Martin Luther, the great reformer, initially felt troubled by life's weights. God's love appeared to be an impossible affection to attain. In reading Romans, Galatians, and Ephesians, Luther also came to the conclusion that his initial view of God's grace and compassion was too small. Still others, such as John Calvin and John Wesley experienced conversion when dwelling in the book of Romans. In fact, Wesley's heart was strangely warmed while reading this theological masterpiece.

St. Paul wrote Romans about twenty years into his ministry. It's no wonder why a deepened reflection of God's character is articulated. He wrote this while he was doing ministry in Corinth. He had planned to visit the believers in Rome — a church that he did not establish. Some scholars speculate that this church began on the day of Pentecost. There is a reference in Acts 2, that Roman citizens were also gathered that day for celebration. It is theorized that they were empowered by the Holy Spirit to return to Rome and formulate a church.

The book of Romans begins with the first few chapters explaining the brokenness of this world and our sinful state of being. In the chapters to follow, Paul reminded us of the story of Abraham and his growing awareness of God's gracious love. Abraham grew in his understanding of God's character. God called him when he was seventy-five years of age. He dropped everything and began to follow this God who was calling him forward on life's journey. God promised that he would give him a child. He would have descendants as numerous as the sands on the seashore, and the stars in the sky. Yet, year after year passed. Abraham and Sarah had waited so terribly long for the fulfillment of God's promises, they began to doubt and question the character of God. Finally, when Sarah was over ninety years of age Isaac, which means "laughter," was born. Abraham was close to 100 years of age. He waited 25 years for this promised child to be born. It says in verses 19 through 21:

> He did not weaken in faith when he considered his own body, which was already as good as dead (for he was about a hundred years old), or when he considered the barrenness of Sarah's womb. No distrust made him waver concerning the

20

promise of God, but he grew strong in his faith as he gave glory to God, being fully convinced that God was able to do what he had promised."

Perhaps Abraham didn't get to that point of deepened trust until after Isaac was born. This miracle child revealed to him that God keeps promises. God is *always* faithful. The promise would be fulfilled. We are all children of Abraham. We are the descendants as numerous as the stars and the sands on the seashore. When God asked Abraham to sacrifice Isaac, he did not waiver at that moment in his trust in God. Abraham at this point in the journey, knew that God is a miracle worker. God would provide the perfect sacrifice.

God provided for Abraham. God also would provide the perfect sacrifice in the New Testament — the Lamb of God. Jesus would fully encounter human suffering, sin, and evil powers. This is a comforting reminder. When life's journey becomes overwhelming, when we become "stuck" in a faith crisis, we are reminded that God is not distant. Where is God in the midst of our suffering world? God fully and deeply enters into our sin stained world on the cross. Jesus holds great power to heal, transform, and resurrect us to new and abundant life.

Paul would later remind us in Romans 8:38, "for I am convinced that neither height nor depth nor anything else in all creation will be able to separate us from the love of God which is in Christ Jesus our Lord." God is much bigger, greater, loving, and compassionate than we can ever fathom. Abraham learned this to be true. Some of the greatest theologians in church history found Paul's writing to affirm this notion of a faithful God that extravagantly loves us.

In reflecting about Abraham and that his wife's name was Sarah, there is a friend of mine named Sara that went through a faith crisis. Sara is another cyclist that was going through a mysterious health challenge. The doctors were baffled and had no idea how to treat her condition. She was unable to live the active lifestyle she enjoyed. Despite fervent prayers, it seemed like the heavens were silent. In despair, Sara told me, "Karna, God has forgotten me. I am not even on God's radar anymore." Her heartfelt confession was brutally honest. Despite the depths of her sorrows, we prayed together. By God's sheer grace, the illness eventually dissipated. Sara was able to return to an active lifestyle that she enjoyed. In reflecting back on that time, she would confess today, "I realize now that we are never off God's radar."

We are *never* off God's radar. What a helpful thought. God is so full of compassion and love. Sometimes, we do find ourselves stuck on life's journey. When I was immobilized on my bike last summer, I didn't know what to do. Thankfully, I wasn't alone. Another cycling friend knew what to do and helped me fix the bike. We continued and finished the cycling race.

On this journey of life we also never go it alone. God faithfully journeys with us. God promises never to leave us or forsake us. When the world is full of chaos, divisions, and concerns, remember that our God is much bigger and greater and more loving and compassionate than we can ever fathom. God keeps promises. God's love comforts and empowers us to be renewed in our own faith. We are propelled forward to encourage others in this journey as well. God is always thinking of you. May God reassure you of this, and rekindle your faith. Amen.

A Love That Heals Divisions

For the message about the cross is foolishness to those who are perishing, but to us who are being saved it is the power of God. For it is written, 'I will destroy the wisdom of the wise, and the discernment of the discerning I will thwart.' Where is the one who is wise? Where is the scribe? Where is the debater of this age? Has not God made foolish the wisdom of the world? For since, in the wisdom of God, the world did not know God through wisdom, God decided, through the foolishness of our proclamation, to save those who believe. For Jews demand signs and Greeks desire wisdom, but we proclaim Christ crucified, a stumbling-block to Jews and foolishness to Gentiles, but to those who are the called, both Jews and Greeks, Christ the power of God and the wisdom of God. For God's foolishness is wiser than human wisdom, and God's weakness is stronger than human strength.

This past year, I've been trying to catch up on pop culture by watching the Marvel movies in chronological order. One of the first main superheroes that people are introduced to is Captain America. This character began as a scrawny kid who desperately wanted to serve his country during World War II. Yet, every time he applied to serve, every branch of the military rejected him based on his wimpy appearance. His motivations were pure and full of integrity. Eventually, a scientist discovered his sincerity and offered him an incredible opportunity — transforming him into Captain America. This science experiment completely changed him into the strongest and fastest military superhero. He became a nationwide celebrity.

Later in the marvel series, there is a particular Captain America movie called, *Civil War*. As the marvel universe continues to tell the story, other superheroes are introduced such as Ironman, Spiderman, and Black Widow. A controversy arises causing these superheroes to turn on each other in an epic battle. Instead of using their gifts to bless the world, they are caught in their own divisions and beliefs about how best to use their powers. In truth, it was painful to witness them fight each other. All of their gifts were designed to bless others.

In today's world, we have divisions all around us. Sometimes these divisions are helpful. Sometimes life can be organized in certain ways to allow for productivity and clarity. A city planner might have divisions of different quadrants. The community may be structured by Northwest, Northeast, Southwest, and Southeast. This helps you get your bearings straight.

Another type of division might be a personality inventory such as the Myers Brigg or The Four Tendencies. There are different types of people in the world. In studying these personalities, it helps us understand ourselves and others better. This is a helpful division.

One of my favorite divisions is a tool from our Methodist friends called the "Wesleyan Quadrilateral." In this tool, there are four quadrants of consideration in discerning a path forward. These areas include: tradition, scripture, reason, and experience. All of these categories are considered when discerning God's desires.

Usually, when we hear the word, "division," we hear a word that is hurtful and harmful. Sometimes, the division can even be to a boiling point. This is what prompted St. Paul to write his letter to Corinth. Paul explained in the first chapter, that the church was divided:

> *I appeal to you brothers and sisters by the name of our Lord Jesus Christ that all of you be in agreement and that there be no divisions among you but that you would be united in the same mind and same purpose. It has been reported to me by Chloe's people that there are quarrels among you, my brothers and sisters. What I mean is that each of you says I belong to Paul or I belong to Apollo's or I belong to Cephas, that is Peter or I belong to Christ. Has Christ been divided? Was Paul crucified for you? Or were you baptized into the name of Paul?"* (1 Corinthians 1:10-13).

In other words, Paul was saying that they were divided amongst themselves. Only one group identifies Christ as their leader. In future verses, Paul shares an interesting quadrant of divisions. Verse 22 and 23 state that "Jews demand signs and Greeks desire wisdom. But we proclaim Christ crucified, a stumbling block for Jews and foolishness to Gentiles. But to those who are being called both Jews and Greeks, Christ the power of God and the wisdom of God" (1 Corinthian 1:22-23). Paul is making an argument that there are various people with varying motivations. As he described this, I envision a quadrant of divisions like this:

1

Jews: Demand signs	Greeks: Desire Wisdom
Jews: Stumbling block	Greeks: Foolishness

In this first quadrant, Jews are demanding signs. What kind of signs were they looking for? They wanted verifiable proof that Jesus is the Messiah. In the gospels, even John the Baptist questioned if Jesus was the Messiah or if they should keep looking. Jesus assures that he is providing miracles, healings and setting captives free.

Likewise, the disciples also questioned Jesus on when he would restore the kingdom of Israel. They had a very specific expectation on what the Messiah would accomplish. Jesus affirmed that he was the Messiah when he asked his disciples, "Who do people say that I am?" (Matthew 16:15). Peter was the one that said, "You are the Messiah" (Matthew 16:16). Jesus assured that Peter would be the rock upon which the church would be built. However, Jesus went on to share with them that the Messiah must be handed over and crucified. Peter wanted to stop this. He couldn't imagine the Messiah being crucified. Jesus responded that Peter was being a stumbling block as he said,

1   This is effective to show this visual on a screen and also on a piece of paper as you hold it up and reference it.

"Get behind me Satan" (Matthew 16:23). It's amazing that one moment Peter was the rock upon which Christ built the church. In a flash, he then became the stumbling block. Jews demanded signs, yet when the sign of the cross was given, this was indeed a stumbling block.

John's gospel offers a series of signs. These signs are markers identifying Jesus as the long awaited one. Finally, Jesus offered verifiable proof that he had victory over death when he raised Lazarus from the grave. The miracle of the raising of Lazarus also created a wave of new followers. Later, when Jesus was in Jerusalem about to celebrate Passover, we heard of the Greeks who, "wish to see Jesus," in the twelfth chapter of John. They were looking for wisdom and answers. They were looking for a powerful leader. Jesus' reputation had spread so far that even Greeks were curious.

When events turned and Jesus went to the cross, all abandoned him. Jews believed their expected Messiah was a failure as they desired a political revolution. Greeks viewed the cross as foolish, for what would they do with a leader that was dead? Yet, we know there was more to the story. There were Jews and Greeks that discovered the power of God.

Paul reminded Corinth of the power of Christ on the cross. Do you know what motivates God? *Love* is God's motivation.[2] Paul wrote in the twelfth chapter that the body of Christ was divided. While there were divisions and quarrels, the entire body and all of its parts had significance. In the thirteenth chapter Paul said: "Listen I will show you a more excellent way…love is patient love is kind love is not envious or boastful or arrogant or rude it does not insist on its own way preserves all things bears all things hopes all things *love never ends*…faith, hope, and love abide; these three and the greatest of these is love."

We need faith this side of heaven as we go about our journey in a broken and sinful world. We need a hope that gives us a sense of resiliency amidst struggles. But love — love will be all that remains. Love is the greatest because in the kingdom of God, love is all that will be in eternal life. Paul wrote later in Galatians, "there is neither Jew nor Greek slave or free male or female but all are one in Christ Jesus" (Galatians 3:28).

2   Cross-fold illustration: At this point, take the piece of paper with the "quadrants" of Jews and Greeks and fold it slowly. With the text inside, fold vertically first. Then fold 2/3 of the way down. Take the folded edge to make a triangle to the top of the flap. Then take a scissors and cut the paper from the bottom up to the top corner. The cut should be an inch in width. As you continue to talk about the love of God, finally reveal by opening the paper that is now in the shape of a cross. The divisions are gone through the power of the cross.

All divisions dissipate through the power of the cross. Jesus entered deeply into the divisions, into the wounds of this world. Jesus heals and holds us with a loving embrace from the cross. The power of the love of God, this expansive love on the cross, reaches out to the whole world. This was encouraging to the community of Corinth. They needed to be reminded of that gospel truth.

Paul continued that we have a calling to share this love with others. He wrote in verse 26 of chapter 1, "consider your own call brothers and sisters not many of you were wise by human standards. Not many were powerful. Not many were of noble birth, but God chose what is foolish in his world to shame the wise. God chose what is weak in the world to shame the strong. God chose what is low and despised in the world things that are not, to reduce to nothing things that are so that no one might boast in the presence of God."

We still live in a broken and divided world. The cross reminds us that the love of God can transform us and heal our divisions. We worship a God of forgiveness. We are Christians, little Chris's, bearing the image of God in the world. We love and serve the neighbor in need.

At the end of the *Captain America: Civil War* movie, he wrote a very heartfelt letter to Iron Man. "Cap" said that they were family. They needed to forgive one another. They were called to use their gifts in the world to bless others.

There is a lot of pain in our world and in our country. These separations are very real. As Paul wrote this encouraging letter to the Corinthian church, what kind of letter would you compose to someone with whom you've felt division? As a spiritual practice this week, consider composing a letter or a prayer journal entry that extends a healing embrace. Even if this letter is never shared with anyone else, there is power in naming the wound and allowing God's love to extravagantly pour over you as a healing balm. In Christ, we are all made whole. God bless, Amen.

An Unconditional Love

You were dead through the trespasses and sins in which you once lived, following the course of this world, following the ruler of the power of the air, the spirit that is now at work among those who are disobedient. All of us once lived among them in the passions of our flesh, following the desires of flesh and senses, and we were by nature children of wrath, like everyone else. But God, who is rich in mercy, out of the great love with which he loved us even when we were dead through our trespasses, made us alive together with Christ — by grace you have been saved — and raised us up with him and seated us with him in the heavenly places in Christ Jesus, so that in the ages to come he might show the immeasurable riches of his grace in kindness towards us in Christ Jesus. For by grace you have been saved through faith, and this is not your own doing; it is the gift of God — not the result of works, so that no one may boast. For we are what he has made us, created in Christ Jesus for good works, which God prepared beforehand to be our way of life.

Every year before confirmation Sunday, I have an intentional conversation with each student that is about to affirm their faith in Jesus. During this time, the students will share about their faith and give feedback on the confirmation program. There is also a classic question that I ask each of them. It is not meant to be a trick question, but rather, a very important inquiry. I'm curious if they remember the definition of a certain word. I ask them: "What is grace?" The majority will respond in one of two ways: Grace is a name. Grace is something that you say before you eat a meal. Their tone indicates that they aren't really sure as they respond with hesitation, as if it is a question returned.

If you were to ask my family, whenever they hear the word, "grace," they think of both a meal and a person. There is a classic scene in the movie, *Christmas Vacation*, where eighty-year-old Aunt Bethany is asked to say grace before their dinner. She is elderly, hard of hearing, and she responds, "Grace, she passed away thirty years ago." When further probed to offer the blessing, she then responds with the pledge of allegiance. Anyone who has viewed this clip can detest that the word "grace," brings laughter and comic relief.

Grace is a *relational* term. The first twelve years of my life, I was convinced that Grace was a person. Grace was the name of the neighbor across the street from me in childhood. She was a sweet, plump, elderly woman who resembled Mrs. Claus in appearance as well as demeanor. Her door was always open. The smell of fresh baked cookies lingered in her kitchen at all times. Her smile, listening ears and welcoming presence relayed to me that I was truly loved and embraced. When I began confirmation classes, I was amazed to discover that grace is also a theological concept of God's lavish love and forgiveness. Still to this day, when I hear the word "grace," I often think of a welcoming elder who is ready to listen and love me unconditionally.

The word grace may conjure up all sorts of images and concepts. Humanity struggles with the nature of grace. This may be due to the reality that grace is often so unexpected, undeserved and unbelievable. Throughout the history of the church, and even today, grace is a rich relational term that challenges us. We may find grace difficult for a variety of reasons.

One reason why grace challenges us, is because it is *undeserved*. It is easy to prematurely judge others. We assume that God's forgiveness could not extend beyond a certain parameter. A purity and desire for sincere devotion may sometimes lead us to a zealous behavior.

St. Paul grew in his understanding of God's grace based on his own personal experience with forgiveness. Prior to his conversion, Saul found grace to be rather difficult to comprehend. Although he believed his motives were pure and well intentioned, he couldn't imagine that the Messiah had come through Jesus Christ. As one who studied the law deeply, there was also a narrow understanding of what the Messiah was sent to accomplish. Extending grace to Gentiles was not initially on his radar. He felt compelled to keep his Jewish faith pure and undefiled, promoting the law and tradition. Upon meeting Jesus on the Damascus Road, Saul experienced lavish grace first hand from Jesus. Grace was not designed for exclusivity. God desires for the whole world to discover this lavish love. Paul's experience of divine forgiveness inspired him to write Ephesians 2:8, "for by grace you have been saved." This particular Bible verse would inspire generations of believers through the centuries.

Martin Luther chewed on this verse that nourished his soul and began a reformation. Luther lived in an era in which *perfectionism* seemed to be the prerequisite to getting God's favor. This was reinforced when indulgences were sold. The church taught that salvation was based on merit. This was certainly not helpful. Human beings carry the weight of the law constantly. Are any of you perfectionists? Do you have incredibly high expectations of yourself? Martin Luther was so inspired by the discovery of grace. This changed the trajectory of the church. Many people struggle with grace due to perfectionist tendencies. Hearing the story of Martin Luther is a refreshing reminder that we are set free.

Maybe your struggle with grace has everything to do with a *sinful past*. Have you been broken by life's circumstances? Have you had incredibly difficult chapters in your life that you feel unworthy of forgiveness? If this is where you are coming from, you may be able to relate to John Newton. When he was a little boy, his mother had prayed and dreamed that one day John would enter the ministry. However, she would never see her child grow up. His beloved mother died when he was only four years old. This experience of intense grief caused John to question God's goodness and love.

In adulthood, John became involved with the slave trade. John was one of the harshest captains. His crew feared him. John struggled with alcoholism and anger. One night, a violent storm at sea caused John to pray. Miraculously, he and his crew survived the storm. When he landed, he changed his life. John left the slave trade and entered into the ministry. He would later write a poem that became a familiar song — "Amazing Grace."[3]

When I ask students, "What is grace?" occasionally there is a shining star that may rattle off the famous acrostic: God's Riches at Christ's Expense. One of the bright student's one year was a youth named Rachel. Her family was very involved in church life. Later that school year we had a youth event. This was a retreat that included service projects, worship and Bible studies. As we were fasting to raise funds and awareness of food insecurity, I assumed when leading a Bible study that I would get a very different answer to a question I posed. We were studying Matthew 25 where Jesus explained that when we feed the hungry, we feed Christ. When I asked the students, "what are

---

3   It is effective to lead the congregation in singing the first verse of "Amazing Grace," together at this point in the message.

you hungry for?" I expected them to say "cheeseburgers," or "pizza." Rachel, the student with incredible depth said, "I am hungry for forgiveness." The whole room went silent as we pondered this truth. We were all hungry for the amazing grace of God. Grace and forgiveness is the universal hunger.

Like Paul, we discover that grace expands beyond any limitations we place. Like Luther, we discover that we can be set free from the chains of perfectionism. Like John Newton, we are reminded that no matter where our past has taken us, God always has a hopeful future. God wipes our slate clean. When I think of the word grace I think of both the prayer and a person — the person we know in Jesus Christ. His arms are wide open to us, as outstretched on the cross. His body and blood are also here on the altar, given and shed for you. Are you hungry for grace today? You've come to the right place. You are loved, forgiven and freed. Amen.

A Love Becoming

So also Christ did not glorify himself in becoming a high priest, but was appointed by the one who said to him, 'You are my Son, today I have begotten you'; as he says also in another place, 'You are a priest forever, according to the order of Melchizedek.' In the days of his flesh, Jesus offered up prayers and supplications, with loud cries and tears, to the one who was able to save him from death, and he was heard because of his reverent submission. Although he was a Son, he learned obedience through what he suffered; and having been made perfect, he became the source of eternal salvation for all who obey him, having been designated by God a high priest according to the order of Melchizedek.

Remember the classic question adults often ask children? The common inquiry is: "what do you want to *do* when you grow up?" When I was a youngster, one of my responses was, "a pastor." After worship on Sundays, I would preach to my stuffed animal collection and play church. At a very young age, I wondered if God was calling me into ministry.

Recently, my eleven-year-old nephew challenged this common question. He is an old soul and a brilliant kid. As he was "graduating from elementary school," he was asked by his class to offer an inspiring speech. Cullen began by stating, "When adults asked us, 'what are you going to *do* when you grow up,' that was not a good question. A better question is, 'what are you going to *be* when you grow up?' What kind of human *be*-ing will we *be*come? What kind of values are they teaching us? Will we *be* kind? Will we *be* helpful?" Assuredly, my nephew had his entire class thinking on a deeper level.

Cullen's insights are inspiring. By asking the question of *being*, rather than just *doing,* this leaves a holy space for God. This is a sacred opening to discern what God is doing in our lives and in the world. Often, we may jump into our days ready to accomplish everything on a checklist. This is a common approach to life. In the business world, I often describe this as a deliberate strategy. In this mode of operation, you set a goal and all the steps to achieve your desired outcome.

A holy and emergent strategy is counter intuitive. This takes a step back and poses the question, "who are you calling me to *be*come God? How might I *be* a reflection of your love in this world today Lord?" This is much more like a surfer catching a wave and noticing the energy of the Holy Spirit calling us to respond to needs in the world. We make God's desires our agenda. We create space to listen and then respond.

In Psalm 46 for example, a lot of activity happens. Mountains crash. The world is in chaos. Verse ten gives us insights: "Be still and know that I am God." The Hebrew for, "*be* still," can also be translated as, "let go." Let go and surrender to God's plans. *Be* still and trust that even when the world is swirling in chaotic confusion, God is still sovereign. All shall be well. In this grounding of a deepened prayer life, after listening deeply to a God of grace and loving power, we emerge ready to serve. Listening to God and tuning out the distractions empowers us to then enter into the busy world and offer God's grace to others.

This prayerful life was deeply modeled by Jesus during his earthly ministry. In the reading for today from Hebrews, verse 7 states, "in the days of his flesh," that is when Jesus walked on planet earth, "Jesus offered up prayers and supplications, with loud cries and tears, to the one who was able to save him from death." Jesus often arose early to listen and surrender the day to God's plans. Prayer was central at every point in Jesus' earthly ministry. At his baptism, even prior to any accomplishments, Jesus was in prayer when he heard God's affirmation, "You are my Son, the beloved." When Jesus chose the twelve, he spent the whole night in prayer and discernment. Prayer was always a grounding exercise that inspired Jesus to do God's will.

As verse seven used the phrase, "deep cries and tears," sometimes Jesus' prayer life was especially emotionally intense. As I reflected on this, I could easily think of three occasions in which Jesus' prayer life got to this level of intensity. They were in fact, quite critical times in his ministry.

First, Jesus cried deeply and loudly in John the 11th chapter. Remember that verse, John 11:35 "Jesus wept"? This was a deep cry in front of his friend Lazarus' grave. Jesus is severely disturbed and upset by the brokenness and pain of this world. Jesus ached at the sorrow and struggles of this world, and he showed solidarity with his friends in their painful loss. Jesus also would do something drastic to reveal that not even death can separate us from God's reach. Jesus would powerfully raise Lazarus from the tomb after an intimate prayer with the Father.

A second moment of intense prayer occurred in the Garden of Gethsemane. Scripture states that his prayers even created bloody sweat. As Jesus prayed for unity and protection for the church in the garden, his intercessory prayer was most acute on the cross. A third moment of intense prayer happened during the crucifixion. Jesus' first words on the cross was a powerful prayer, "Father, forgive them." In these deep cries and tears, Jesus relayed both the desire to fulfill God's will, and the heart of a humble Lord. This was a ministry of creating space and continual conversation with God the Father and the Son.

In the reading for today from Hebrews, there is also an obscure reference to Melchizedek. You may be wondering who was this priest? He is mentioned again in the seventh chapter, briefly in a Psalm and also in Genesis 14. Melchizedek was both a king and a priest who offered a blessing to Abram. In addition to a tithe, Melchizedek also gave Abram bread and wine. As Jesus is referred to as a priest in this same order of Melchizedek, we also come to the communion table with open hands, ready to receive a nourished blessing from God.

Remember the cliché, "You are what you eat?" When we partake in Holy Communion, we experience the very real presence of Jesus. This love of God is within us. As we reconnect with God and create space in our lives for Christ's presence, we become the tangible hands, feet and voice of Jesus in the world today. Holy Communion recenters us as we experience God's love in the bread and wine.

Jesus' prayer life also inspires us to pause and pray as we begin each day. My nephew truly is a great reminder to all of us: "who are you going to *be*?" You are a child of God. May you trust in this promise that you are *be*loved. You are the body of Christ. *Be* yourself. Trust and know that God hears your deep cries and tears. God bless, Amen.

Liturgy of the Passion
Philippians 2:5-11

The Journey Of Love

Let the same mind be in you that was in Christ Jesus, who, though he was in the form of God, did not regard equality with God as something to be exploited, but emptied himself, taking the form of a slave, being born in human likeness. And being found in human form, he humbled himself and became obedient to the point of death — even death on a cross. Therefore God also highly exalted him and gave him the name that is above every name, so that at the name of Jesus every knee should bend, in heaven and on earth and under the earth, and every tongue should confess that Jesus Christ is Lord, to the glory of God the Father.

World religions have always fascinated me. In my family of origin, there is philosophical diversity. My sweet grandmother was a church organist, but her three sons took various spiritual journeys: Atheism, Buddhism, and my father became a Lutheran minister. Intrigued by humanity and all of the varying ways to understand God, I was delighted to travel as a missionary to India and Nepal after college. It was here that I often asked the question: Why am I a Christian?

One remarkable day in India, we traveled to an extremely remote village. While people and water buffalo overpopulate the land, *remote* simply means that they did not have access to a lot of technology and luxuries. We took a barely discernible path to arrive at our destination. In the distance, we saw men approaching us with sticks above their heads. Confused, we were a bit scared. We wondered if they came with a friendly greeting or potential violence. To our surprise and delight, they started engaging in stick dances around our van. Then they instructed us to sit on top of our vehicle as they led us in a parade through the town. This community had never met Westerners before. It was an exciting moment in their lives! Meanwhile, we felt unworthy to sit atop, as if elevated to a pedestal. This was truly, an unforgettable day when we paraded through this gracious and welcoming village.

As Jesus rode on a donkey, parading through the streets of Jerusalem, I wish I could hear the thoughts of the crowd that day. Many wondered if this was the Messiah who would overturn the Roman government. Perhaps others in the crowd experienced healing from Jesus or a miraculous feeding. What were the disciples thinking as Jesus humbly and peacefully rode into town? What's more, how was Jesus processing this experience? Jesus knew this week would be a journey from cheers, jeers, tears and cheers once again. In other words, Jesus loved us so much; he did not remain on this pedestal the whole week. Love would stoop down. Love would have a very definable journey of great depths and heights.

Love would come down and meet us in our darkest sorrows and deepest pains. Love would come down and kneel at our feet. Love would wash the very feet that followed him for three years. Love would offer a meal to all gathered in the upper room — even though all would fall short and betray him. Love would surrender to a higher will and not let the cup of suffering pass from him. Love would be arrested, tried, tortured and crucified. Love would come down to the depths of hell and total darkness. Love would do this for you, for me and for the whole world. Love would then rise above the clouds and embrace a hurting world with arms outstretched. Love would resurrect and offer a larger view of hope and expansion. There is always more to the story. Love would sink down, but love would also rise higher than we ever imagined possible.

While journeying through India, the reality of a gracious and loving God became ever apparent to me. I had asked one of our missionary teammates that grew up in India, "as you've been surrounded by so many faiths all your life, why be a Christian?" She shared that when she was a teenager, a missionary had preached of a deep love that came down. Yet, this love didn't stay down. As the world fixated with a lens downward, they stumbled in the darkness. All they needed to do is look up. The brilliant light of Jesus was shining and guiding the way. This love and light would reveal a greater compassion and healing power the world craves.

While we felt unworthy to sit on top of our vans and parade through a village in India, we were grateful for this warm welcome. In truth, many days in life, we humans can feel discouraged and doubtful. As we begin Holy Week, it is encouraging to recognize that wherever you find yourself on the journey of life, Jesus travels alongside you. Holy Week compresses all of the turmoil and triumphs of life. As Jesus rode humbly into the heart of the city, he came in peace and with power.

Do you feel discouraged today? Do you feel as if you long for a hope that can transform your life and this world? Do you feel abandoned and angry? Are you hoping for a reminder that tomorrow can turn the pages of you life's story around? Jesus assures us that there is nowhere we can go in which we are out of the gracious grasp of God. You are loved. You are known. You are not alone on your path of life.

This reading from Philippians reminds us that the journey of love has a path: to find you and meet you where you are. It was originally also a song of hopeful praise. When we recognize that Jesus meets us on this journey, and that love comes directly to us, this song of lament turns to a major key. The melody of love begins to ring in our ears and is the cry of our hearts. This was the love that my missionary team sang about to the remote village in India. This is the love that we sing about today.

We have a God in Christ that is so intimately attentive to our journeys. Whether we find ourselves in the depths or in the heights, love leads and lights the way. Jesus would humble himself and be raised again as the great name that holds power. The grace and love of Jesus assures us that wherever our journeys take us, we are not alone. While love comes down to meet us, love also raises us with a hopeful view. God is always with us on our journey. May you trust and know that you are not alone. Christ loves you and leads you. All shall be well. Amen.

A Love That Calls You By Name

For I received from the Lord what I also handed on to you, that the Lord Jesus on the night when he was betrayed took a loaf of bread, and when he had given thanks, he broke it and said, 'This is my body that is for you. Do this in remembrance of me.' In the same way he took the cup also, after supper, saying, 'This cup is the new covenant in my blood. Do this, as often as you drink it, in remembrance of me.' For as often as you eat this bread and drink the cup, you proclaim the Lord's death until he comes.

One of the most comforting sounds to my ears is the voice of my mother. Her voice resonates a tone of compassion. I love it when she calls me by name. As a youngster, I remembered playing outside in the sandbox or climbing a tree. While I would be enjoying a time of play, three words would cease activity and I'd come running home. It wasn't the three words, "I love you," but it could be mistaken as such. Instead, it was this phrase, "Karna, dinner's ready!"

While my mom has a sweet-toned voice, her cooking is also unmatched. I knew that there was a place for me at the table. I knew by her labor of love over a home-cooked meal that this would nourish my soul. When I moved away in college years, mom would always answer the phone with the kindest voice, "Hello, Huh-Hagen's" Our last name always managed to catch another syllable when she spoke. It was so comforting to me that mom was always home waiting and still calling me by name to this day.

These childhood memories translate to the hunger we all share. To be called by name and invited to a meal of grace is a deep hunger of our souls. It is a gift to know that even when we are busy with worldly joys and distractions, our God welcomes us back and invites us to the table. While there is an incredible longing to taste grace, isn't it interesting that whenever we think about the night Jesus shared this meal with his friends, we refer to it as, "The night in which he was betrayed." Certainly betrayal happened. All of the disciples would fall short and turn away. John the beloved witnessed him die on the cross. He was also powerless to prevent this event. Art depicts John as the disciple who leans in closely to Jesus to hear the heartbeat of God. It is no wonder then, why John refers to himself as the *beloved* disciple. What would happen if we lean in closely and listen to what Jesus said in words and actions that night?

Yes, it is the night Jesus experienced betrayal from others. Yet, from Jesus' perspective — it was also the night in which he clearly demonstrated there really is no greater love than this. This was the night Jesus revealed, on a deeper level, the great gift of forgiveness and love. Taking the form of a slave, he washed their stinky and filthy feet. The dirtiest parts of us, the very parts of us that we are most ashamed of, Jesus would purify and love. Jesus would pour out wine and bless bread to reveal that he was willing to die for the salvation of the world.

Have you ever wondered what it would be like to experience Holy Communion in that sacred space with Jesus and his disciples? This reading from 1 Corinthians reminds us of two simple words that personalize this meal: *for you*. Jesus would do all of this *for you*. Although all of them would fall short, Jesus would still feed the disciples and offer a meal of grace. Jesus would also feed Judas who shared the bread with him, revealing that he would offer compassion to the one who would hand him over to death. In denial, betrayal and death, Jesus offers love. This was the night Jesus would share a sacred meal and reveal grace and love *for you*.

We may hear these words, *for you*, but still find it difficult to comprehend. Maybe you feel spiritually hungry, but you are uncertain of where you will experience this loving welcome of God. Maybe you are carrying heavy burdens and shames that weigh you down. Maybe you've felt hurt by the world, or the church, and you do not hear the words, *for you* as clearly as they are spoken. Maybe you just can't get past the words, "on the night in which he was betrayed." The betrayal, denial, and distance from God feels like a chasm that cannot be bridged.

While Jesus said the words, *for you*, the good news is that God knows you by name. You are not a number to God. You are not unknown. There's a pastor I know who once told me an incredible true story from his ministry. I happen to call him, "Pastor Daddy," and he refers to me as "Pastor Daughter." While my dad was greeting people on a Sunday morning for worship, a visitor mustered the strength to walk through the doors of the sanctuary. This man looked like he graduated from the school of hard knocks. His life was full of chapters of grief, struggles, and shames. This visitor wanted a fresh clean start to life. The trajectory he had been on didn't work for him anymore.

As he approached "Pastor Daddy," he revealed, "Pastor, my name is Paul and I'm a broken man." My dad sensed that Paul was looking for a gracious God that would remember his sins no more. As Holy Communion was blessed later in the service, there was both a written and verbal invitation, "all are welcome to the table of grace." The bulletin stated this welcome. The words were spoken. My dad looked at Paul while this invitation was spoken. Pastor Daddy's eyes were full of compassion.

A miracle happened that day. Paul who hadn't braved crossing the doors of a church in 25 years, stepped forward. He kneeled and opened his hands to receive an incredible grace from God. Words were spoken that deeply inspired his soul, "This is the body of Christ given for you — Paul." At the sound of his own name, Paul recognized the very real presence of Jesus in his life. He was called, claimed and loved by God. Paul went home that day and opened up a dusty old Bible. Words from the pages of scripture pierced into his heart that he is a beloved child of God. He also would later find himself at another dinner table.

Whenever holidays would come, my gracious mother would think about who to invite to the meal. As I sat next to Paul, I had never witnessed someone so thankful to be known, loved and invited to the table. In Holy Communion, God calls your name too. Just as my mom's comforting voice chimes, "Karna, dinner's ready," trust and know that our Lord Jesus remembers this as the night of revealing a deeper love from God. In fact, Maundy is the Latin word for "mandate," the command to love one another. Let us reflect this love of God in the world. Keep inviting people to the table. All are hungry. All are welcome. Amen.

Good Friday
Hebrews 10:16-25

A Love Amidst Life's Questions

'This is the covenant that I will make with them after those days, says the Lord: I will put my laws in their hearts, and I will write them on their minds', he also adds, 'I will remember their sins and their lawless deeds no more.' Where there is forgiveness of these, there is no longer any offering for sin. Therefore, my friends, since we have confidence to enter the sanctuary by the blood of Jesus, by the new and living way that he opened for us through the curtain (that is, through his flesh), and since we have a great priest over the house of God, let us approach with a true heart in full assurance of faith, with our hearts sprinkled clean from an evil conscience and our bodies washed with pure water. Let us hold fast to the confession of our hope without wavering, for he who has promised is faithful. And let us consider how to provoke one another to love and good deeds, not neglecting to meet together, as is the habit of some, but encouraging one another, and all the more as you see the Day approaching.

Years ago, I recollect a conversation in a pastoral care class at seminary. When life doesn't make sense, or when people are going through a horrific ordeal, we were advised not to ask any "why," questions. On a pragmatic level this seemed to make sense. As I pondered, "why not ask why?" it occurred to me that "why" leaves you spinning in circles. There never seems to be closure and satisfaction in any answer that you hear. "Why?" puts people on the defensive.

Yet, if we are being honest, we ask this question often anyway. "Why do bad things happen to good people?" Sometimes this question is also asked out of sheer curiosity and a desire to grow. In fact, I think of the question, "why," every year on Good Friday. This very basic question of longing reminds me of an inquisitive and innocent little girl.

This child was a second grader. She was visiting her grandmother for the Easter weekend. As she hadn't worshiped very often in her short little life, she happened to have a pen and a little notebook. Instead of drawing pictures during worship — this little one wrote down every question she could think of about Good Friday. After worship, she insisted that her grandmother find me because, "she had a lot of questions!"

As the second grade student pulled out her note pad, she began by asking, "Why is Friday called, 'good.' Why did Jesus have to die? How was Jesus God and human at the same time?" As she began asking question after question, a crowd of adults started to listen in on the conversation. One middle-aged man stated, "That's a great question!" Adults were now surrounding us as this inquisitive little one drew us all in with her desire to understand God.

Satisfied with my answers, the young second grader nodded in understanding. It was then that I asked her, "What's your name?" She exclaimed, "Phoebe!" I told her that was incredible as my cat is also named Phoebe, affectionately named after my favorite character from the show "Friends." Phoebe then told me that she would rename her cat, "Pastor Karna." This child's inquisitive nature was refreshing, but also coming from a place of longing. She wanted a deeper understanding of God and the reassurance that God is truly *good*.

Questions can be helpful. They can propel us along on the journey of faith. It is also extremely comforting to know that even Jesus asked the ultimate question on the cross: "My God, my God, why have you forsaken me?" (Matthew 27:46). The *why?* question is intuitive to ask. We need to ask such questions. Yet, there is wisdom in asking other questions too. If "why" is the only question asked, we may not get to where we want to be on our spiritual journey. We may find ourselves stuck.

On the cross, Jesus reveals a whole breadth of questions. As Jesus asked the question, "why," he answered his own inquiry. The reading today from Hebrews reveals that "by the new and living way that he opened for us through the curtain [that is, through his flesh]"(v.20). The curtain was torn. The chasm between the holy and the human is bridged. This actually changes the question to a better one — *who*. The most important question is *who*? That is, *who* will embrace us, love us, and empower us to be raised to new life? Jesus with arms outstretched loves the world and assures us of an ever-faithful presence.

As we sing together the next congregational song tonight, we too ask a new question: "*What* wondrous love is this?" This is a deepened love that joins us in our sorrows and raises our spirits to new life. This is a love that finds us, holds us ever close, and heals our brokenness. This hymn also sings, *"when* I was sinking down…" in the depths of life's valleys, Jesus' arms extend to pull us up out of this sorrow. *Where* does this happen? Right here, and right now, we know that the Holy Spirit is inspiring us. *Why* leads us to **who**, *what, when* and *where. How* is still a profound mystery that God would take on flesh, live among us, die, and rise again? *How* also propels us forward as we look to God with great mysterious awe.

Hebrews reminds us today of the importance to continue gathering as a worshipping community. The Good News of Jesus, the **who**, that holds us, gives us a "hope without wavering for he who has promised is faithful" (v. 23). God is faithful. God meets us in our questions, fears, doubts and chaos. The curtain is torn. The love of God has free roam to access us and assure us of this extravagant love of God. To continue hearing this message of salvation and grace keeps us steadfast and confident. We may have questions, but Jesus is the answer to calm our fears and fill us with faith. Jesus is our **who**, that holds us ever close.

This childlike curiosity keeps us going in our broken world. These questions of the faith continued to inspire Phoebe years later. She returned to live with her grandmother during her high school years. Although life has its challenges for all of us, there was something about this Jesus that continued to draw her close to the fold. It is the goodness of God that reminds us why we call it "Good Friday." The aches and questions in our souls are satisfied in another question: **who**. May you trust and know that Jesus is a faithful Lord that meets you in your swirling questions and doubts. Nothing can ever separate you from this mysterious and perfect love. Thanks be to God. Amen.

Resurrection of the Lord
Acts 10:34-43

An Extravagant Love ForThe World

Then Peter began to speak to them: 'I truly understand that God shows no partiality, but in every nation anyone who fears him and does what is right is acceptable to him. You know the message he sent to the people of Israel, preaching peace by Jesus Christ — he is Lord of all. That message spread throughout Judea, beginning in Galilee after the baptism that John announced: how God anointed Jesus of Nazareth with the Holy Spirit and with power; how he went about doing good and healing all who were oppressed by the devil, for God was with him. We are witnesses to all that he did both in Judea and in Jerusalem. They put him to death by hanging him on a tree; but God raised him on the third day and allowed him to appear, not to all the people but to us who were chosen by God as witnesses, and who ate and drank with him after he rose from the dead. He commanded us to preach to the people and to testify that he is the one ordained by God as judge of the living and the dead. All the prophets testify about him that everyone who believes in him receives forgiveness of sins through his name.'

Christ is risen! Christ is risen indeed! Alleluia! Happy Easter to all of you. As we proclaim the resurrection so clearly here today, will you share this hope outside of this place? God's love for the whole world is extravagant. This message is meant to be shared. The world is full of people aching to experience God's love.

Many feel rejected, broken, isolated, and confused. There is a spiritual hunger and thirst for God. There is a universal holy hunger to know that we are **loved**. The entire world is a mission field. If you had the chance to share your faith with someone longing to hear good news, what would you say? Who is someone you know that is longing to hear a word of grace and inclusion? Who is someone you know that experienced brokenness from life's circumstances? Is there anyone in your life that might be open and curious to hear about God but they've had no exposure to the Gospel?

When I was 23-years-old, I traveled as a missionary to India and Nepal. As our seven-member team trekked through the Himalayan Mountains on the Anna Purna range, we came to a place where there was an entire gathering of people that had *never* heard the story of Jesus. They had no idea what was in the Bible. One of them asked us, "Will you tell us the whole story of the Bible?" Without skipping a beat, one of our enthusiastic teammates began detailing highlights of the Bible narrative with incredible storytelling! As this group heard the story of creation, the fall, families in Genesis, Exodus, Kings, Prophets, and Exile, all leading up to the promised Messiah, you could hear a pin drop. The story of Christ's birth, ministry, death and resurrection stirred a realization of a loving and welcoming God that would embrace them fully. They were inspired!

In this Bible reading today from Acts, we hear Peter's first sermon to a Gentile community. To appreciate and understand the full scope of his message, the backdrop provides needed context. The entire tenth chapter of Acts reveals that Peter experienced an incredible spiritual revelation. As one of Jesus' closest disciples, Peter *still* had new insights to learn about God's heart. As Peter grew in his understanding of God's extravagant love for the world, his purpose and message transformed.

> *Acts 10 begins with the story of a centurion named Cornelius. Acts 10:2 reveals so much about Cornelius' character and spiritual hungers: "He and his family were devout and God-fearing: he gave generously to those in need and prayed to God regularly." Pausing here, we have learned so much about this Cornelius. Although he is a Roman centurion, he is leaning into God. His family also shares in this faith. Cornelius is devoted in putting his faith into action by learning about God, giving out of his abundance and growing spiritually through his prayer life. If you recollect, there were other centurion's that also showed a spiritual curiosity during Jesus' ministry. One trusted that Jesus could heal his servant at a distance (Luke 7:1-10) and of course there was the curious on-looker at the foot of the cross stating, "Truly this was the Son of God" (Matthew 27:54.)*

Cornelius' prayer life was especially attuned to the Holy Spirit's guidance. While he was praying, God revealed to him that a man named Peter would come and minister to him. At this same time, Peter is also deep in prayer. God gives Peter a vision to kill and eat unclean animals. Peter is startled by this request, until God reveals that Peter should not describe what God has made as unclean. Peter was challenged to open his heart to embrace all animals, and also to embrace all humans.

By the time Cornelius and Peter meet, we discover that Peter has grown in his understanding of God's extravagant love. The gospel is inclusive. Peter's first words in his sermon state that he realized God shows no partiality. God does not play favorites. All are welcomed into this embracing fold of God's love. This is such a helpful reminder for us today. It is so timely to hear that God does not favor various people. The message of salvation is for all people of all time. This extravagant love of God is expansive and inclusive.

Peter also states in his first sermon to Cornelius and company in verse 36, "You know the message he sent to the people of Israel, preaching peace by Jesus Christ — he is Lord of all." Did the phrase, "preaching peace," grab your attention? What does this mean to "preach peace?" Perhaps you recollect the Hebrew word, "shalom." Variations of this word are often used as greetings in this region of the world. Its deeper meaning is "wholeness and wellness." Preaching peace means proclaiming the good news of whole-heartedness. That is, we offer the compassion and blessings of God to a world fractured by anxieties.

This is what it means to "preach peace." It is to know that we are fully and lavishly loved by God and to allow this grace to spill out of us and into the crevices of this world where the gospel has not yet been proclaimed. Is there someone in your life who has not yet heard this good news of God's inclusive and extravagant love? How might we as a congregation be inspired to embody this loving presence of God in the world today?

There was a young girl named Chass. She had not experienced a world of peace and God's love. Her parents struggled with drug addictions. Chass often felt alone and afraid. God found a way through the everyday folks in her small town to reveal a greater love. Every church in town, Methodist, Lutheran, Presbyterian, Reformed, Assembly of God, and more, took turns hosting a Vacation Bible School.

Chass' parents thought this would be great "free babysitting." Every week, Chass was dropped off at a new church and surrounded by devoted Christians who "preached peace." For the first time in her life, she experienced an extravagant and radical divine love. This changed the trajectory of her life.

Chass began praying for her parents at a young age. During her teen years, her parents also experienced a miraculous liberation from the addictions that had bound them. Later, Chass would study to become a missionary to India and Nepal. She could not keep this good news of Jesus to herself. Chass was my best friend from high school. She had a profound impact on my life. When I had the opportunity to travel to India and Nepal as a missionary, Chass told me, "the whole world is a mission field. Everyone is hungry for the love of Jesus. Go and tell others this great news!"

Peter proclaims that all are included in God's loving embrace. Let us preach peace to an anxious world. Who is someone you know that needs to hear this good news of God's great love? Perhaps it is you who needs to be reminded. May you trust and know this extravagant love of God is for you and for all people. May we also be emboldened to share this divine love in words and actions to a hungry world. Christ is risen! Christ is risen indeed! Alleluia!

A Love That Shines

We declare to you what was from the beginning, what we have heard, what we have seen with our eyes, what we have looked at and touched with our hands, concerning the word of life — this life was revealed, and we have seen it and testify to it, and declare to you the eternal life that was with the Father and was revealed to us — we declare to you what we have seen and heard so that you also may have fellowship with us; and truly our fellowship is with the Father and with his Son Jesus Christ. We are writing these things so that our joy may be complete. This is the message we have heard from him and proclaim to you, that God is light and in him there is no darkness at all. If we say that we have fellowship with him while we are walking in darkness, we lie and do not do what is true; but if we walk in the light as he himself is in the light, we have fellowship with one another, and the blood of Jesus his Son cleanses us from all sin. If we say that we have no sin, we deceive ourselves, and the truth is not in us. If we confess our sins, he who is faithful and just will forgive us our sins and cleanse us from all unrighteousness. 10 If we say that we have not sinned, we make him a liar, and his word is not in us. My little children, I am writing these things to you so that you may not sin. But if anyone does sin, we have an advocate with the Father, Jesus Christ the righteous; and he is the atoning sacrifice for our sins, and not for ours only but also for the sins of the whole world.

Have you ever felt alone, isolated and longing for authentic community? Perhaps you felt this when you moved to a new town. Maybe you were looking for real meaningful connections with others when you began a new job. For those that have studied at college, this can also be that time when everything and everyone is new. There is a deep ache to belong.

When we brought our nephew André to his freshman year of college, he was so full of anticipation. André grew up in Mexico. When he studied for his senior year of high school in Minnesota, he stayed in our home. As a dual citizen, he was invited to arrive early to bond with other international students before the entire class would arrive.

We were told that international students often come with two suitcases from the airport. Bedding would be provided for them as well as other essentials.

With this knowledge, we assumed that bringing André to college wouldn't take long. We packed hiking shoes to explore the campus and trails nearby. However, once we got to Decorah, Iowa, we discovered an urgent problem. Andrés international cell phone had no signal amidst the bluffs and cornfields of northeastern Iowa. The closest store to remedy the situation was 140 miles away round trip. We knew that a working cell phone offered security and community. Without a phone, no one could communicate with him. This was a safety concern. There were no landlines in the dorm rooms. A working cell phone was also a necessity for building community and friendships with other students on campus. We couldn't imagine leaving our nephew alone and vulnerable. After multiple hours of driving, we remedied the situation.

In our high-tech world, it's hard for us to imagine the context that John the beloved disciple experienced. Historically, we know that he was banished on the island of Patmos. Traditionally, he is thought of as the inspirational author of the gospel of John, the letters of John and Revelation. As I know his story of isolation on an island, I've often pictured him writing in seclusion. With this image of his home office space of solitary island confinement, it is holy ground that he had the ability to describe this extravagant love of God.

As this first letter begins, John is focused not only on the love of God, but a light that shines brighter than any darkness. Verse 5 specifically states, "God is light." What does this mean? What does light do and how does this correlate with what God does?

One property of light is very obvious: it helps us see. Light gives us vision. Similarly, God also gives us guidance in our lives, offering navigation on where to take our next steps. Light also gives us clarity. John the beloved disciple had a deepened insight into the extravagant love of God.

Light is also energy. This energy fills us with resilience. When it is dark in the wintertime in Minnesota, a happy light immediately fills our brains with joy. God also uplifts our spirits when we are weighed down by the darkness of our sins. The forgiving power of God's light shines on our brokenness, restores us, and motivates us to a newfound purpose. We are made alive in Christ.

While sight and resilient energy are interesting correlations between light and God, there is a third property of light that I find very interesting. Light provides warmth. Sitting by a campfire, it is fascinating to watch the fire dance above the logs. Underneath, there are also extremely hot coals. Kept together, this heat from the coals provides the ideal temperature to cook food. The warmth of light also serves as a metaphor for the compassion of God.

When I think about John the beloved disciple, I'm in awe. Perhaps he studied campfires on the beach of Patmos. In this time of isolation, he reflected on how God is light. However, a closer look at the first verse reveals insights. Did you notice the plural language here? In the first verse of first John it says, "We declare to you what was from the beginning, what we have heard, what we have seen with our eyes, what we have looked at and touched with our hands." Who is the "we?"

Is it possible that this plural language is John's kinship with the Holy Spirit? John is known as the disciple who leaned so closely to Jesus during the Lord's Supper that he heard the very heartbeat of God's compassion for the world. This is a possibility.

Scholars debate on the authorship of these letters. It is also quite possible that this was written by a Johannine *community* that knew deeply the theology that John articulated. This inspired community knew that they were called to be a very real, tangible presence of God in a dark world. The church is called to shine.

When people are seeking a new church, this is often during a time of transition. Perhaps they moved to a new community and they long for authentic friendships. Some experienced pain from a previous church so they pursue a new gathering where they can find acceptance. During a time of great grief, some may begin to ponder the bigger questions of life. While God is truly light, Jesus reminds us that we are also light. A city on a hill must shine.

Our mission at Our Savior's states that we are a "caring community, called by Christ to serve and live in faith." The loving warmth of God is stated directly in our mission to be a caring community. Recently, we had the opportunity to do this. A few weeks ago, a high school student tragically died. Though Isaac was not a member of our congregation, many of our youth knew him well. The family thought to ask our church, "May we use your Christmas Eve candles for a community prayer vigil?" My response was, "Absolutely."

The family didn't know how many to expect at the outdoor vigil. They guessed that maybe 300 could show up. I'm also not sure how many candles we have in stock. I would guess around 500-800. The night of the prayer vigil, 1,500 people showed up! We quickly ran out of candles. A friend of mine later noticed that many of our staff and I were in attendance. She wondered, "Was Isaac from Our Savior's?" I shared that he was not, but he has many friends from our church that knew him well. This is what we do and this is who we are. We show up. We are light. We share the light of God.

As we all gathered, on a golf course, shining the light of Jesus in this dark world, we were in awe at the turnout of caring people. We saw God's love. We were uplifted with resurrection hope as the lights burned brilliantly. There was an obvious *warmth* from the wider caring community of Stillwater, Minnesota.

God is light. You are light too. On Christmas Eve, when we receive the light for our handheld candles, we are reminded to also *share* the light. We are called to both *be* the light and *share* this light of God to a world that longs for Christ's love. The warmth of loving Christian community transforms the world. "Let your light shine before others, that they may see your good works, and give glory to your Father in heaven"(Matthew 5:16). God bless, Amen.

A Love That Claims And Names Us

See what great love the Father has lavished on us, that we should be called children of God! And that is what we are! The reason the world does not know us is that it did not know him. Dear friends, now we are children of God, and what we will be has not yet been made known. But we know that when Christ appears, we shall be like him, for we shall see him as he is. All who have this hope in him purify themselves, just as he is pure. Everyone who sins breaks the law; in fact, sin is lawlessness. But you know that he appeared so that he might take away our sins. And in him is no sin. No one who lives in him keeps on sinning. No one who continues to sin has either seen him or known him. Dear children, do not let anyone lead you astray. The one who does what is right is righteous, just as he is righteous.

Have you ever held a newborn baby? Parents, grandparents, aunts, and uncles alike find this to be a truly holy experience. Whenever we hold a little one in our arms, questions of possibility flood our brains. What does this child's future hold? What kind of personality will they develop? What kind of chapters will their life's story tell? As children grow, parents learn to let go for a stretch when they enter school. This is especially true when this little one leaves the nest altogether to venture to college or other life adventures.

My parents tease that although they are not "baby boomers," they have "baby boomerangs." That is — they send their kids into the world, but the kids always come back to visit. Whenever we leave the house, even to this day, my mom quotes her favorite movie from 1985, *Witness*. This film stars Harrison Ford and details his character's interactions with an Amish community. The Amish grandpa said to him, "Now you be careful out there among them English." My mom is known to quote this to us each time we fly the nest after visiting.

This phrase seemed to indicate to me, "Don't forget your roots." "Be true to yourself." "The world can be a tough place, so come back to us in one piece." There was one time, however, that my mom didn't say this to my brother. She was much more direct that day. My brother recollects that this was the hardest day of his life. It was after 9/11 when the twin towers were attacked. His wife Cristina desired to move back to her home country of Mexico. She had already flown to her home city, and she was waiting for him there. Meanwhile, my brother would have to drive their mini-van from Minnesota to southern Mexico.

On that day, my mother could see Ethan's sadness. He was truly leaving his roots. As a loving parent, she looked him gently in the eyes, put both of her hands on his shoulders and said to him as her voice cracked, "Never forget who you are. Ethan James Hagen, child of God." She couldn't be more clear.

John is clear as well in this first letter. "See what love the Father has given us, that we should be called children of God; and that is what we *are*" (1 John 3:1). We so easily forget our true identities as beloved children of God. It's as if we embark on life's highway, and the vehicle in front of us has debris that cracks our windshield. Looking through the shattered glass, we cannot see ourselves, the world or even God clearly. This contorted view begins early in life. We drive along and a classmate teases us. We continue the journey and a teacher remarks on a paper that we think is a defining moment. We audition for the team or the play and do not get the part. We define ourselves by success. We discern that our failures determine our worth. We keep driving life's highway, looking to see who we really *are*.

This first letter of John clearly states who we are: loved children of God. While this is obvious and a reminder of what we know, this message does not always resonate deeply in our bones. How did John hold such confidence in this identity? I believe that it is the latter verses here today that offer us clarity and insights into how we may fully affirm God's name and claim. It is the tension between the word "sin," and "abide."

First, the word "sin," in Greek is translated in a way that you might find surprising. "Sin," by literal definition is an archery term that means, "missing the target," or "missing the mark." That is, instead of hitting a perfect bull's eye, the arrow lands off-center, off-mark. Sin means that we are not centered in our true identity as children of God. When we are "off-center," and we experience this disequilibrium, we cannot see ourselves, the world and God through an accurate lens. We are simply "off," and "distant," from hearing that affirming voice of God.

This separation from God does not have to be our reality. The word, "abide," reveals another option. "Abide," literally means: dwell, reside, make your home in, even tabernacle. It is the same word that you find in the upper room narrative where Jesus encourages us to abide, dwell, live richly with God. The translation "tabernacle," really catches my attention. It is so comforting to know that on life's "highway," we have a God that journeys with us always. Just as God was with the Israelites in the wilderness, this presence of God, this tabernacle, remains with us no matter where life's road leads.

The story of Joseph from the Old Testament is a great example of God's faithful presence abiding. In his early years, Joseph defined himself by his colorful coat. This affirmation from his father was what he needed as he would face a lifetime of pain and pure joy. As his envious brothers sold him into slavery, destroyed his coat and claimed that he was "dead," Joseph embarked on an unexpected journey. At every turn, whether favorable conditions or extreme hardships, the scriptures reveal a very comforting notation: "the Lord was with Joseph."

Joseph is sold into slavery by his brothers — but the Lord was with Joseph (Genesis 39:2). He found favor with Potiphar — The Lord was with Joseph (Genesis 39:3). He was falsely accused and put into prison. The Lord was with Joseph (Genesis 39:21). His gift of dream interpretation led him to be second in command in Egypt. The Lord was still with Joseph. This presence of God dwelling with Joseph and his awareness of God's grace softened his heart. By the time he and his brothers reconnect and reconcile, Joseph *changed*. His brothers were new creations too. This is what it means to *abide.*

Never forget who you are — a beloved child of God. This is something I also teach at pre-baptism classes. I tell parents to make the sign of the cross on their infant's foreheads each night and say, "Jesus loves you and so do I." This is reminding children from the get-go that they are named and claimed by God.

One Sunday, a grandpa approached me with tears in his eyes, "my twin grandkids just blessed me last night. Apparently you taught their parents five years ago to do this bedtime routine. Now they bless their parents too. They blessed me last night."

Never forget who you are — a beloved child of God. You've been sealed with the Holy Spirit and marked with the cross of Christ forever. May you trust and know that you are named and claimed. God's love dwells within you. God is with you wherever you go. Amen.

Love Is A Verb

We know love by this, that he laid down his life for us — and we ought to lay down our lives for one another. How does God's love abide in anyone who has the world's goods and sees a brother or sister in need and yet refuses help? Little children, let us love, not in word or speech, but in truth and action. And by this we will know that we are from the truth and will reassure our hearts before him whenever our hearts condemn us; for God is greater than our hearts, and he knows everything. Beloved, if our hearts do not condemn us, we have boldness before God; and we receive from him whatever we ask, because we obey his commandments and do what pleases him. And this is his commandment, that we should believe in the name of his Son Jesus Christ and love one another, just as he has commanded us. All who obey his commandments abide in him, and he abides in them. And by this we know that he abides in us, by the Spirit that he has given us.

Ten years ago, I was working out at the gym when a couple of friends approached me with what they described as an important question: "If you could have a meal with anyone in all of human history, who would you choose as your dinner date?" One of the friends, an agnostic, spouted off a variety of historical figures he found fascinating. I thought about this question for days. They insisted I had only one choice. Would I want to eat a meal with my grandma in heaven? Would I choose a famous celebrity, past or present? I told them I would get back to them on my answer in a couple of days.

As I continued to wrestle with this question of whom I would choose as a dinner date, something completely unexpected happened. It was late October on a Thursday morning. The temperatures were beginning to drop to single digits. This is not uncommon for Minnesota. As I was working on my Sunday sermon, a mom and her three-year-old daughter walked right into my office. Before the mom could say one word, the little girl noticed a fun sized bag of Cheetos on my dorm fridge in my office. She walked right up to the fridge, grabbed the chips and immediately started eating.

"Sarah, stop!" The mom called her daughter's name. "I'm so very sorry..." Before the mom could say another word, Sarah noticed a cookie too. "Can I have 'dis?" The adorable little one looked her mother in the eyes. Then Sarah noticed a fresh stick of gum on my desk, "Can I have 'dis too?"

It was so obvious to me. Sarah and her mother were homeless. Sarah was in fact starving. As the temperature was nine degrees outside, they were only wearing dirty hoodie sweatshirts. My heart sank. I knew that their needs were genuine. Thankfully, this church had just collected winter coats for families in need. We had a clothing store on site where people could pick items they needed. We also had a food shelf right in the congregation's kitchen as well. Sarah and her mother came to the right place. I offered prayer shawls for the mother and daughter to help keep them warm. At this, the mom called her fiancé on her cell phone exclaiming, "Honey, you'll never believe it! I'm at a wonderful church. They are going to help us."

Perhaps this was my answer to the question, "who would I share a meal with?" Sweet little Sarah, a precious three-year-old, ate a portion of my lunch that day. This also reminded me of these powerful words from *1 John 3:17-18: How does God's love abide in anyone who has the world's goods and sees a brother or sister in need and yet refuses help? Little children, let us love, not in word or speech, but in truth and action.*

In truth, I sat there awestruck and motionless as a toddler hungrily gobbled down my meal. Thanks to the ministries of the congregation I was serving, this family found clothing, food, and connections with an organization called Family Promise that empowers families to find their way out of a poverty cycle with stable housing and employment opportunities.

This church had the world's "goods," and was poised to share abundantly. At Our Savior's we also have a grace fund to help members in need. In addition, we have a mission and outreach fund that distributes 11% of our collected offerings each year to organizations that help the hungry and homeless.

John's letter reminds us that love is not just a concept or a feeling. Love is a *verb*. Faith in action is vital to demonstrate God's love to a hurting world. What if my door had been closed? What if the church had no compassion or resources? Jesus reminds us in Matthew 25:35, "I was hungry and you fed me." At the same time, Jesus recognizes that *we* are hungry too. Sometimes we are paralyzed to move and put our faith into action. We find ourselves stuck because we need the re-assurance that we are truly loved, forgiven, and freed to serve.

Jesus knows this. Love is a *verb*. As John's letter reminds us of this incredible commandment of God to love others, Jesus instituted this in the upper room. Do you need some healing and refreshing water to cleanse your sins? Love is a *verb*. Jesus washes our feet and takes our sins away. Are you hungry for a meal that will last? Love is a *verb*. Jesus gives his very self in the body and the blood.

The disciples in the upper room had difficulty digesting the meal and the message. They were full of anxiety, wondering who would betray Jesus. Peter didn't want Jesus to stoop so low as to wash his feet. In this emotionally charged room, they were so overcome with fear and finger pointing. They had no idea what would happen in the coming days.

Love is a *verb*. Jesus would pray in the garden. Love is a *verb*. Jesus would carry a cross. Love is a *verb*. Jesus would die to take away the sins of the world. Jesus would give his life away, as food for the hungry. Each week as we participate in Holy Communion, we recognize that love is a *verb*.

Which leads me again to answer the question: "Who would I want as my dinner date?" The other friend that posed this question was a member of my church. He said, "I always wanted to be there the night Jesus gave the disciples communion. Now that I know the whole story, I think that I would appreciate it even more as I would know what was coming next. I can't imagine how much love I would feel from Jesus. He was doing this for the whole world, and for *me*."

Here's the Paschal mystery. Each time we do have Holy Communion, this meal transcends time. It connects us with the saints that have gone before us. We remember "the night in which he was betrayed." It is a foretaste of the feast to come — so that I do have communion with my heavenly grandparents. This meal connects us with believers across the globe. When we receive this body and blood, Christ truly abides in us. We become bread for the hungry. We are the Body of Christ in a hungry world. This empowers us to serve and share of our abundance with others — including sweet three-year-old girls who hungrily gobble down our lunch.

Love is a *verb*. The church is God's tangible presence on earth, poised and ready to serve. Who would you share a meal with this week? How might all of us be bread for the hungry? As you receive

Holy Communion today — may you clearly hear the affirmation that you are deeply and perfectly loved by God. May Christ compel us to share that same love with a world so hungry for good news. God bless. Amen.

God Is Love

Beloved, let us love one another, because love is from God; everyone who loves is born of God and knows God. Whoever does not love does not know God, for God is love. God's love was revealed among us in this way: God sent his only Son into the world so that we might live through him. In this is love, not that we loved God but that he loved us and sent his Son to be the atoning sacrifice for our sins. Beloved, since God loved us so much, we also ought to love one another. No one has ever seen God; if we love one another, God lives in us, and his love is perfected in us. By this we know that we abide in him and he in us, because he has given us of his Spirit. And we have seen and do testify that the Father has sent his Son as the Savior of the world. God abides in those who confess that Jesus is the Son of God, and they abide in God. So we have known and believe the love that God has for us. God is love, and those who abide in love abide in God, and God abides in them. Love has been perfected among us in this: that we may have boldness on the day of judgment, because as he is, so are we in this world. There is no fear in love, but perfect love casts out fear; for fear has to do with punishment, and whoever fears has not reached perfection in love. We love because he first loved us. Those who say, 'I love God', and hate their brothers or sisters, are liars; for those who do not love a brother or sister whom they have seen, cannot love God whom they have not seen. The commandment we have from him is this: those who love God must love their brothers and sisters also.

I met my greatest spiritual teacher on my first day of kindergarten. Before entering the classroom, my mom instructed, "Karna, there is going to be a very special girl in your class. I want you to be good and kind to her. I want you to be her friend." In my innocence, it was unclear to me what my mom meant. My ears heard, "mom wants me to have the special friend!"

As I peeked inside the classroom, boys were on one side playing Legos and girls were segregated in another play area. In the middle of the room, I immediately noticed a classmate that was sitting on the floor and dribbling a basketball. "Only big brothers know how to dribble! She must be the special friend." We introduced ourselves to each other. She invited me to her home that day and I had my first Mountain Dew and fruit roll-up.

Kristin could swim and read by the age of three! She had an endless amount of toys. She accepted everyone in the class. No one was a stranger. Everyone was truly loved by Kristin. Yet, not everyone reciprocated this love to her.

A year later, I realized what made Kristin so special. Bullies were teasing her on the playground one day. That's when I heard the word, "Down Syndrome," for the first time. I prayed to God that day that I would always be her friend. Even when I moved away in high school, Kristin and I kept in touch. In fact, she was the maid of honor at my wedding.

"Perfect love casts out fear," John tells us in verse eighteen today. Fear is commonplace in today's culture. Many fear those that they do not know or understand. This anxiety and fear creates unnecessary divisions. Humans rank and exclude others. If you are beautiful, athletic, wealthy, and smart you are deeply accepted. Humanity shuns certain people groups for their gender, sexual orientation, race, religion, politics, age, social status and a variety of other factors.

With all of this fear of the neighbor unknown, how do we bridge the gap and love as Jesus commands us to do? If Jesus spent so much of his time with people in the margins of society, why is there such a disconnect between Jesus' mission and the church's embrace of all? Fear seems to beget more fear. Love multiplied transforms our environments.

Jesus drew crowds wherever he ministered. He spent long days healing the sick, feeding hungry, and letting the little children come to him. When others feared and shunned lepers, Jesus was unafraid to touch the "unclean," and restore them fully to physical and social well-being. In John 4, Jesus intentionally traveled to Samaria to meet a woman at a well who was a social outcast. He took this path to make it abundantly clear that he meant what he said in John 3:16 in the previous chapter, "For God so loved the world that he gave his one and only Son, that whoever believes in him shall not die but have eternal life."

On the cross, Jesus fully embraces the entire world, offering a healing posture. There is a profound mystery of the cross. On the cross,

Jesus embraces the whole world — both the persecuted and the perpetrators. There is a transformative healing juncture that occurs that brings reconciliation and healing to all. God is love. There is no fear in God to embrace all that was made. God is love. God reaches out to all of us to hold us ever closely. God embraces our sins, fears and wounds. Thank goodness that God is love. No one is ever turned away from the embrace of God. All are welcome into God's loving and healing arms. This is good news for me, for you, and for those that we might find a hard time embracing.

While God's love is perfect, how can we even try to love like Jesus? This was the very question a young woman named Thérèse asked daily. She was only fifteen years old when Thérèse felt the call from God to join a convent in Lisieux, France. She had this profound understanding that God is love. She assumed that the convent would be a community of enriched spiritual friendships. Instead, Thérèse was shocked that some nuns were unloved by others, rejected and shunned socially. This revelation caused Thérèse to question her calling.

She turned to scripture for the Holy Spirit's guidance. 1 Corinthians 12 detailed the Body of Christ. Thérèse knew she wouldn't be the voice of God, she was not allowed to preach. She could not be the hands of Christ, she was not allowed to administer the sacraments. As a cloistered nun, her calling was not to be the feet of Jesus. As she continued to read 1 Corinthians 13, she remembered "a more excellent way." She wondered if anyone had chosen to be God's heart. That was her calling!

Thérèse developed what she called *The Little Way*. Her calling was to seek out the most marginalized at the convent, and assure them that they knew God's heart was big enough to embrace them fully. In the next century, Dorothy Day and Mother Teresa found Thérèse of Lisieux, to be their inspiration to embrace the world's outcasts. In fact, Mother Teresa, changed her name from Anjezë to honor her spiritual hero.

It is *The Little Way*. It is baby steps. It is small gestures and kind smiles that soften hardened hearts. It is seeking out the lonely and forgotten with intention that demonstrates "God is love," to a population that may question this notion. *The Little Way* need not be a grandiose plan. Rather, it is small steps of openness to embrace what God already adores.

The Little Way was my prompted approach to meeting my greatest spiritual teacher, Kristin. My mother instructed me to look for a very special girl in my class. Kristin's compassion for others resembles *The Little Way*. I never forgot who bullied her on the playground. Kristin had no recollection of the event. She called these former bullies friends!

Kristin and Thérèse of Lisieux were coming from a place of knowing first that they are deeply loved by God. "We love because he first loved us" (1 John 4:19). My spiritual director once asked me, "Karna, when your mother told you that there would be a special girl in your class and that you should be good and kind to her and be her friend, did you ever think that this girl was *you*?"

God is *love*. When we experience that profound love of God, this transforms us. When we practice *The Little Way* and really take note of our environments, embracing all, this transforms our world. God is love. We are also Christ's body on earth, called to love like Jesus. In the coming week, I encourage you to explore *The Little Way*, and see what happens. You may be amazed at the transformation that will take place in you and others. God bless, Amen.

Love One Another

Everyone who believes that Jesus is the Christ has been born of God, and everyone who loves the parent loves the child. By this we know that we love the children of God, when we love God and obey his commandments. For the love of God is this, that we obey his commandments. And his commandments are not burdensome, for whatever is born of God conquers the world. And this is the victory that conquers the world, our faith. Who is it that conquers the world but the one who believes that Jesus is the Son of God? This is the one who came by water and blood, Jesus Christ, not with the water only but with the water and the blood. And the Spirit is the one that testifies, for the Spirit is the truth.

When I was a youngster in Sunday school, I remembered learning a song that taught, "Love one another, love one another, love one another Jesus said." This command is easier said than done. How do we love *everyone*? Sometimes, it's challenging to love those in our own *household*. When I was born, my Grandma Hagen said that I "broke my brother's nose." I had no idea what this meant. Ethan, who is four-years-older than me always seemed jealous. He held a grudge when we were little. At that time in life, we didn't get along. It was years later that I realized what my grandmother meant. We had sibling *rivalry*.

In today's reading, John states, "everyone who loves the parent loves the child" (1 John 5:1). While I love my brother, it was challenging to treat one another with kindness. The dividing line of couch cushions could not be crossed while watching Saturday morning cartoons.

This division experienced so innocently in childhood is magnified in our wider culture today. Separations, jealousy, misunderstandings and even violence overwhelm us. Social media reinforces our own echo-chambers, creating even greater divides. Polarizing politics make civil conversations difficult to experience. How do we live into the song, "Love one another"?

Perhaps the third verse today requires deepened reflection: "For the love of God is this, that we obey his commandments. And his commandments are not burdensome" (1 John 5:3). In the first part of this verse, we should pause at the word "commandments." Perhaps when you hear this word, "commandment," you recollect the Ten Commandments that were given to Moses. Our relational Triune God cares deeply about our personal connections.

All of the Ten Commandments emphasize how we may enhance our interpersonal relationships. The first three commandments begin with a focus on our relationship with God: love God fully, honor God's name, and delight in God by keeping the Sabbath holy. Out of our abundant and grace-filled relationship with God, we learn how to love others around us. In fact, the very next commandment continues with the first relationship we are introduced to in our lives: our parents. The last seven commandments then, detail how we may flourish in our human interactions. Honoring and respecting others also comes back to us four-fold with blessings.

While the Ten Commandments are meant to empower us to flourish in all of our relationships, they are obviously impossible to keep perfectly. Did you also notice in John's letter today that he referred to these commandments as if they are *not "**burdensome**"*? As I've been reflecting on this verse, the word "burdensome," grabbed my attention. At times, "burdensome," is an apt word choice to describe exactly how challenging it is to love others for whom we have difficulties. "Burdensome," also reminded me of another powerful encounter someone once had with Jesus as they conversed about commandments.

Remember the rich young ruler who posed the question to Jesus: "Good teacher, what must I do to inherit eternal life?" (Luke 18:18). Jesus answered that every commandment must be obeyed perfectly. This young man is convinced he has already accomplished this on his checklist. Jesus then looks at him with compassion and tells him the one thing he cannot do: give away everything he owns to the poor. This was a very wealthy man that Jesus was instructing. Ironically, the one "lack" he had was that he did not "lack," the blessings of this world. This young ruler walked away feeling that this law, this instruction, was *"**burdensome**."*

Jesus was conveying a very valid point here that this young man missed: ***grace***. Did you notice that the rich young ruler asked, "What must ***I do*** to inherit eternal life?" This question stems from a faulty premise. If you begin at the wrong start, the trajectory and logical conclusion will be misguided. Jesus is saying that the ***only*** way to inherit eternal life is ***through the grace*** of God. It is through the love Jesus would demonstrate on the cross.

On a similar occasion, an expert in the law tested Jesus by asking the same question: "what must *I do* to inherit eternal life?" (Luke 10:25). Here, Jesus sums up the law "Love the Lord your God with all your heart and with all your soul and with all your strength and with all your mind, and love your neighbor as yourself" (Luke 10:27-28). Pressed further, this lawyer then questioned who was considered to be our neighbor? Jesus continued by sharing the story of the Good Samaritan.

Two correlations in these stories found in Luke are: God's ***grace*** and ***compassion***. We are clearly saved through the grace of God. We cannot earn our way to salvation. God's compassion is also evidenced by these stories as well. God cares about the poor, the broken, and the marginalized. God challenges those who assume they are greater, too busy or apathetic to the needs of the world.

This still brings us to the question: how do we love one another? Is there a way to develop the capacity to love those for whom we find it quite difficult to embrace? Is there a pathway to expand our hearts to love like Jesus? Is there a way for us to practice loving ourselves, our neighbor and God at a greater intensity? While we are not capable of perfecting the law, and thank goodness our salvation is not dependent upon this, there is a spiritual practice that I have found incredibly helpful. This is called *The Loving Kindness Meditation*.

My doctoral work included a compassion retreat for Our Savior's Lutheran in which participants combined a practice of *The Loving Kindness Meditation* and *The Little Way* of St. Thérèse of Lisieux. When practiced daily, there is an inner shift that takes place to enlarge one's heart for self, God and others. *The Loving Kindness Meditation* is a spiritual practice that is found in many religious traditions, including Christianity.

The Loving Kindness Meditation is essentially a ripple effect of blessings for self and others. You begin by offering compassion for yourself. You know all of the hardships and joys you have faced in your life. As you close your eyes and breathe deeply, you gently offer yourself blessings of: health, happiness, peace, joy, and love. After you bless yourself, think of someone you dearly love. Picture sitting across a table from them. Then offer your loved one the same blessings of: health, happiness, peace, joy, and love. This process continues as you think of someone for whom you have neutral feelings, an acquaintance, and strangers. If possible, you also extend blessings to people that you find challenging and for all beings everywhere.

While these blessings may not change someone else, this prayer time has the capacity to transform *us*. We experience this compassion of God personally. It is out of that abundance that we share Jesus' embrace with the world around us. This is a spiritual practice I have personally used to bless others that I have found challenging. By God's grace, I found peace to handle the daily encounters with them, even if the environment remained the same.

"Love one another," Jesus commands us. Is this a possible command to obey? By God's *grace*, absolutely. A miracle happened when my oldest brother Eric went off to college. My dad told my mom, "You watch Kathy. When Eric goes off to college, I predict that Ethan and Karna will become very close." My dad was right! Something like scales fell off both my brother Ethan's and mine eyes. We saw each other in a new way. We are brother and sister. Today, I never even think about the early childhood years when we didn't get along. He's my brother. We deeply love each other. May our world experience a profound healing that comes through God's grace. Let us overflow and share this love with one another. God bless, Amen.

A Life Of Love

If we receive human testimony, the testimony of God is greater; for this is the testimony of God that he has testified to his Son. Those who believe in the Son of God have the testimony in their hearts. Those who do not believe in God have made him a liar by not believing in the testimony that God has given concerning his Son. And this is the testimony: God gave us eternal life, and this life is in his Son. Whoever has the Son has life; whoever does not have the Son of God does not have life. I write these things to you who believe in the name of the Son of God, so that you may know that you have eternal life.

What do you think of when you hear the word, "testimony?" Maybe you love television shows with court cases. Hearing the testimony from the witness stand draws us into examine the evidence for the case. In a church context, the word "testimony," conjures up an image of an enthusiastic new believer or traveling evangelist. During the Lenten season, it is also not uncommon to hear someone's faith story and how God is working in their lives.

When I hear the word "testimony," I have a very special image in my mind. Several years ago, a friend of mine confessed that he was a recovering alcoholic. He invited me to attend an open AA meeting stating, "This might help you professionally to know what my peers and I have experienced." This was a type of meeting where friends who are supportive of those in recovery were encouraged to attend.

When I arrived, I was blown away by how much this seemed to resemble a loving and healthy church. There was authenticity and welcome. We began the meeting with the serenity prayer. Then, multiple people went into great detail of how they hit rock bottom and discovered a high power, God, that miraculously healed them. They could not stop telling their stories and encouraging others to work the steps. They cared for one another deeply, reminding each other of the profound difference God made in their lives.

In the reading today, John reminds us that God is life. "And this is the testimony God gave us eternal life, and this life is in his Son.

Whoever has the Son has life; whoever does not have the Son of God does not have life" (1 John 5:11). God offers abundant and eternal life. This is something that John personally witnessed as a disciple of Jesus.

In the Gospel of John, we notice several unique stories of people transformed by their encounters with Jesus. A woman caught in adultery also finds life in Jesus as he rescues her from being stoned to death. Mary and Martha are forever grateful for Jesus' powerful raising of their brother Lazarus from the grave. God is both abundant and eternal life.

A man born blind experienced healing from Jesus. John's Gospel takes the time to unpack his story throughout the ninth chapter. He discovered a whole new world he can see. God gave him a brand-new life. The Jewish leaders found this to be absolutely remarkable that he could be healed, so they put him and his parents on trial. He shared his testimony. Jesus gave him sight and a new life.

Two beloved stories in John's gospel are found back-to-back: Nicodemus and the woman at the well. I believe this is no accident that we find these two stories next to one another. In doing so, John is making a statement. Nicodemus and the woman at the well are complete opposites in every way possible.

Nicodemus is a scholar, wealthy, influential, male, and named. The woman at the well was uneducated, poor, a social outcast, female and has no recorded name. As a leader of the community, Nicodemus would appear to have all of the answers. Yet, he approaches Jesus by night with an ache in his soul. He was actually spiritually hungry. Meanwhile, the woman at the well was out in broad daylight, with obvious thirsts for divine truths. I fully believe that the deep hole in both of their souls — the profound question that gnawed at their minds — was fully known to Jesus. This is a question that all humanity wonders: Does God really love me?

Imagine Nicodemus' shock when Jesus cuts to the chase and reveals to him, "not only does God love you Nicodemus (oh you who try to uphold hundreds of laws perfectly), but God loves the whole world." Likewise, the woman at the well's soul was stirred to new insights that Jesus deeply loved her — despite knowing her painful past. "Come and see a man who told me everything that I have ever done" (John 4:29).

What a gift it would be to interview Nicodemus and this woman at the well. Their testimonies inspired people in their daily social circles, as well as all of us today. They represent a full spectrum of humanity. They tell the story of how all of us are hungry, thirsty, and questioning God's love. Their testimony reveals that God is *life.* God is both abundant life on earth and eternal life that awaits. Their lives were never the same after encountering Christ.

The same was true for my dear friend. I'll call him "Matthew," which means, "gift of God." His spiritual insights were a cherished present to unpack. Matthew knew such a profound extravagant love. There was no question that God's healing love was vast and abundant in his life. As he brought me to an AA meeting to hear the testimony of his peers, you could hear a pin drop as each told their stories. Every person's testimony shared stories of extreme pain and trauma. Every testimony also shared stories of an extravagant love that called them by name, and rescued them from the depths of hell. Every testimony shared about their own encounters with a death of the old, and a resurrection of a new person. They knew that God is *life.* God is *love.* We have this abundant love and life to share as well.

When the meeting time came to a close, we all stood in a circle on the outside parameters of the room. Holding hands, we recited the Lord's Prayer together. This really felt like church. Matt squeezed my hand at the end of the prayer and whispered to me, "Every person here believes every single word of the Lord's prayer. Without God, we would all be dead. God's love and healing power is real. *Trust God.*"

Matthew's encouragement deeply touched my soul. Here I was, like Nicodemus, a religious leader with profound doubts. "Does God love me? Does my life matter?" These were the aching questions of my soul. At the time I was a single pastor, longing for a life partner. I was convinced that my life could never experience deep joy. I felt alone like the woman at the well. I also struggle with perfectionist tendencies that Nicodemus may have also known. Did God really care about me? Matthew revealed to me, through the testimony of dozens of his friends, the answers to these questions. The last words Matthew ever said to me were, "*trust God.*" I took those words to heart. To my amazement, God also answered the deep cry of my soul and blessed me with a wonderful husband.

God is *life*. God is *love*. God is always at work in each of our lives. What would your life's story tell? What is your testimony? May you trust and know that at the heart of it is a profound love of God who is still writing your story. There are more chapters to write. There are still pages to be written. God bless, Amen.

Day of Pentecost
Acts 2:1-20

Share The Love

When the day of Pentecost had come, they were all together in one place. And suddenly from heaven there came a sound like the rush of a violent wind, and it filled the entire house where they were sitting. Divided tongues, as of fire, appeared among them, and a tongue rested on each of them. All of them were filled with the Holy Spirit and began to speak in other languages, as the Spirit gave them ability. Now there were devout Jews from every nation under heaven living in Jerusalem. And at this sound the crowd gathered and was bewildered, because each one heard them speaking in the native language of each. Amazed and astonished, they asked, 'Are not all these who are speaking Galileans? And how is it that we hear, each of us, in our own native language? Parthians, Medes, Elamites, and residents of Mesopotamia, Judea and Cappadocia, Pontus and Asia, Phrygia and Pamphylia, Egypt and the parts of Libya belonging to Cyrene, and visitors from Rome, both Jews and proselytes, Cretans and Arabs — in our own languages we hear them speaking about God's deeds of power.' All were amazed and perplexed, saying to one another, 'What does this mean?' But others sneered and said, 'They are filled with new wine.' But Peter, standing with the eleven, raised his voice and addressed them: 'Men of Judea and all who live in Jerusalem, let this be known to you, and listen to what I say. Indeed, these are not drunk, as you suppose, for it is only nine o'clock in the morning. No, this is what was spoken through the prophet Joel: "In the last days it will be, God declares, that I will pour out my Spirit upon all flesh, and your sons and your daughters shall prophesy, and your young men shall see visions, and your old men shall dream dreams. Even upon my slaves, both men and women, in those days I will pour out my Spirit; and they shall prophesy. And I will show portents in the heaven above and signs on the earth below, blood, and fire, and smoky mist. The sun shall be turned to darkness and the moon to blood, before the coming of the Lord's great and glorious day.

In the spring of 2007, during my senior year at Luther Seminary, I traveled to visit friends from my internship congregation in Portland, Oregon. Upon the return flight to Minneapolis, I found myself at a layover in the Las Vegas airport. After grabbing a fast food dinner, I sat down to consume my meal while reading a book for class on Christology. As I was wading through thick theological concepts, suddenly, another traveler saw the book I was reading and engaged me in debate. She was convinced that Jesus was not God. Tongue-tied, this soon-to-be-pastor was absolutely speechless.

Meanwhile, another traveler came to my defense and said, "It's one God in three persons: Father God, Jesus God, Hoooooly Spirit God!" I never knew that "Holy" could have multiple syllables. In the midst of this heated encounter, the first lady was still unconvinced and walked away in anger. When the air seemed a bit less tense, another woman approached me and sincerely stated, "I've always wanted to know how it is that Jesus could be God incarnate. You see, I grew up Jewish."

In reflecting on this unexpected encounter, I returned to seminary feeling crushed. Who was I to pursue pastoral ministry? How could God use me to proclaim the good news when I failed to articulate the complexity of the doctrine of the Trinity? Wallowing in grief and fear, I wanted to flee from a future laying on of hands at my ordination.

I was not the first follower of God to be tongue-tied, fearful and full of excuses. Remember the story of Moses? When God called him from the burning bush he was *relentless* that God find *anyone* else. Thankfully, God knew that Moses was perfect for this calling. Moses was the *only* person who knew both Pharaoh's court and the wilderness. His past experiences led him to this moment to lead God's people into freedom.

Our gracious Lord abundantly supplied everything Moses needed. While this included his brother Aaron to be a spokesperson, the real gift was this faithful presence of God. "I will be with you," the great *I AM* stated. God faithfully showed up as a cloud by day and pillar of fire at night. God provided daily sustenance. God's presence was obvious to them in the tabernacle. God showed up every single moment. This presence of God never left their side. It is this same promise that Jesus gave the disciples, "I am with you always to the end of the age."

Although Moses had his own agenda, thankfully, our gracious God fulfilled this plan of liberation and leading a whole nation to a promised land. The journey with God is one of joy, trust, and a pathway to true wholeness. Have you ever envisioned the stories that would *not* be written if everyone in scripture stubbornly refused to walk with God and share their faith?

What if Esther allowed her people to be annihilated from a decree? This would have also ended her life prematurely. What if King David never wrote a psalm of praise or lament that inspires us to this day? What if King Solomon never prayed for wisdom and led foolishly? What if Ruth stayed home and never ventured with her mother-in-law to meet Boaz and become a part of the genealogy of Jesus? Imagine that Mary and Joseph told the Angel Gabriel, "Find someone else to raise the Messiah!" What if Peter stayed home with his wife and mother-in-law and never followed Jesus? What if Mary Magdalene had never known the healing power of Jesus? Where would the world be if Mary Magdalene never came to the empty tomb and became the first follower of Jesus to proclaim the resurrection?

In each of these call stories, fear was a common initial reaction. Many of these ordinary folks wondered how they could possibly be considered a vessel of God's message to a hurting world. When fear tries to overcome us, we may offer excuses that we are: too old, too young, untrained, inexperienced, and the like.

Meanwhile, all God desires is that we are *available*. Even if it resembles Moses' call story, "I'll go, but send my brother Aaron to speak on my behalf." God doesn't worry about our qualifications. God equips each person. As God revealed to Moses, so God reveals to us, "I will be with you." The Creator of the ends of the earth is with us still. All excuses melt away at the mysterious power of the Holy Spirit's fire.

Can you picture the day of Pentecost? As the disciples huddled closely together in anticipation of the Holy Spirit, the entire city of Jerusalem was filled with faithful Jewish residents and visitors from regions far beyond Galilee. Yet, instead of being tongue-tied like I was in an airport debate, the disciples' tongues were loosed with supernatural ability to speak fluently in foreign languages. The diversity of Jerusalem on that day is comparable to an airport today. People from all walks of life are all gathered together. What's remarkable is that there were people in this very city that could clearly hear the Good News of Jesus' victory over the grave in their own language and dialect. All of the known languages of antiquity were represented on that day.

Can you imagine the confidence the Holy Spirit gave the disciples? They were empowered! Translated in today's culture, if all of a sudden

I could speak Chinese, this must be my calling to speak to people fluent in this language. The day of Pentecost, was a day of empowering Jesus' followers to share the extravagant love of God — to people who would then carry this message globally. It was a miracle! The Holy Spirit began with a small few, to multiply the message of God's extravagant love to regions well beyond their initial scope.

Martin Luther calls this equipping from the Holy Spirit the "Priesthood of all believers." We are all called and equipped to share God's love in our daily lives. The word "vocation," comes from the Latin word, "*vocatio*" which means, "voice." We hear the voice of God calling us, whether through burning bushes or tongues of fire, to proclaim God's love in words and actions.

We are called to serve the neighbor right in front of us. Sometimes this looks like listening to a co-worker or encouraging a neighbor. Other times we may share our faith by volunteering in the church or wider community. If we all listened to that voice of God nudging us, we would never need to recruit Sunday school teachers or singers in the choir each fall.

Imagine what the world would look like if we all said, "Yes," and trusted the promise of God, "I am with you." There would be no more hungry or homeless people. We would live in a world where violence is something of the past, and kindness is the norm. We would be inspired to live and give generously of our time, talents and treasures. We would discover an extravagant love that heals us from our brokenness. We would share this love of God in abundance each day. Our world would look a little more like heaven on earth.

As we make ourselves available to God's service, our faithful Lord follows through with the promise of his presence. Five years ago, I again found myself on an airplane. After years of excuses, I finally surrendered to God to pursue a Doctorate of Ministry through Fuller Seminary. My biggest fear was getting off the plane and finding my way through Los Angeles to Pasadena, California. What if I got lost? Would I be safe? Are you sure about this God? I protested in my prayer life.

My fears subsided when I met the passenger sitting next to me. He reminded me of a classmate from Luther Seminary. As I struck up a conversation with him, asking the stranger if we had met before, he responded, "no." Then he asked me, "I get this question a lot and I need to know, is it my beard or my hairstyle that makes me look so familiar?" I studied his face for a few seconds and responded, "possibly both your hair and beard." The passenger said, "That's what I was wondering. You know, a lot of people think that I look like *Jesus*."

When he offered this suggestion, I knew that God really was with me on this journey. This call was out of my comfort zone, but it was not beyond God's ability to provide. God calls each of us to follow in faith. God can use you in your daily life to bring joy, light and Christ's love. You are called. You are equipped. The world is waiting to experience God's love through your presence. Don't worry about what to say or do. God's Spirit will be with you always. God bless, Amen.

About The Author

The Reverend Dr. Karna Moskalik is the Lead Pastor at Our Savior's Lutheran Church in Stillwater, Minnesota. She graduated from Augustana University in 1999 with a major in Communication and a double minor in English and Religion. In 2000, she traveled as a missionary through Youth Encounter to India and Nepal. From the fall of 2000 through the summer of 2003, Karna served as a youth minister at Word of Peace Lutheran in Rogers, Minnesota. Her pastoral internship was at St. Matthew Lutheran in Beaverton, Oregon. She earned her Master of Divinity from Luther Seminary in 2007. Her first call was at Gloria Dei Lutheran in Rochester, Minnesota. In 2020, she earned her Doctorate of Ministry from Fuller Seminary. Her dissertation focused on compassion and resiliency.

Karna was a competitive storyteller in speech during her teenage years. She loves music, particularly vocal and guitar. In her spare time, she enjoys distance cycling, cross country skiing, and watching Dr. Who episodes with her husband Brian. Their favorite vacation destination is the Wisconsin Dells. They are happily married and raising two cats named Shorty and Alex.

www.ingramcontent.com/pod-product-compliance
Lightning Source LLC
LaVergne TN
LVHW011412080426
835511LV00005B/500